PHP

BLUEPRINT

An Essential Beginners Guide
to Learn the Realms of PHP From A-Z

David Mitchell

TABLE OF CONTENTS

Introduction

PHP is considered one of the most popular development languages and web applications. It was created in order to make dynamic Web pages; however, over the years of its existence, the PHP language turned into something much more useful. Thanks to PHP development people can easily create complex applications, such as forums, photo galleries and much more.

This book will introduce you to the process of writing code and developing on PHP language. It will lead along the way from creating a simple web page with content before building interactive web applications.

We will touch upon security issues, interaction with the database, and creating a development environment for your PHP applications. As you read the book, you will be working on a small but reliable blog application to apply theoretical knowledge, obtained in each chapter, to the real development process.

Before starting a merciless fight, it is good practice to get informed and to prepare. As probably said by a very great man whose name I do not know and whose existence I cannot prove, "half the battle is played during its preparation." On the menu of the day, you will find a short introduction to the basics of PHP and especially on the overall operation of it. Everything will be complemented with a few lines on what is programming, and as for dessert, I will let you discover it.

Chapter One

The Basics Of PHP

$\mathbf{B}$efore embarking on scripts, you have to start at the beginning: the syntax of PHP.

This part is essential; if you do not know the basics of language at the fingertips, you will lose a lot of time later.

PHP, The Web, What Is It?

PHP, for PHP: Hypertext Preprocessor, is a programming language. There are many others, like C, Java, OCaml, but we can say that PHP is a programming language oriented for the Web or for websites.

For the record, PHP was born at the hand of RasmusLerdorf in 1994. At first very basic, it was made public in 1995 under the name of PHP / FI. Subsequently, the development passed from the hands of RasmusLerdorf to those of two students - ZeevSuraski and Andi Gutmans - who later founded Zend Technologies to promote PHP. If you develop applications with PHP, you will undoubtedly hear about Zend, whether through their framework, their development environment, or their server, respectively Zend Framework, Zend Studio, and Zend Server.

Not content to be a programming language, PHP is an interpreted language. When you use an application, under Windows, for example, you double-click on the program to launch it; the program then runs, your computer can directly run the program. For PHP, it's a little different. Indeed, your computer does not understand PHP; it does not know how to run it, for PHP to be executed, the file containing the PHP code must be interpreted by ... the PHP interpreter.

In concrete terms, what is the interpreter? As I said, your computer can not run PHP code as it runs a classic application. For your code to come alive, the interpreter - which is an executable application - will read it, translate it into an intermediate dialect - the Opcode - and finally ask your computer to execute the instructions corresponding to the generated Opcode. You will hear again about Opcode in the rest of this book, so do not stop there for the moment, just know it exists.

The Web - How Does It Work?

First of all, what is the Web? The Web - or World Wide Web - is the system that allows you to read this content, which allows you to access content, pages of a site, usually accessible via the internet. The Web is often confused with the Internet, but the Internet is definitely not on the Web: many other systems, applications, and protocols use the Internet. It is quite sad that some entities - companies, for example - rely on this confusion to make more attractive offers; by hammering us with slogans similar to "unlimited Internet" when, in fact, they offer us only access to the web, and still, not always very "unlimited" ... But I go astray; this is not the subject.

The web works on a model in which there are two speakers: the client and the server. You can perfectly make a comparison with a restaurant, it is quite relevant, and it gives good taste. When you are in a restaurant, sitting quietly, you choose a dish, whistle the waiter and tell him what you want. Once the client's request is received, the server will do its internal cooking to deliver what you ordered finally. So there are two messages, first a request from the client to the server, then a response from the server to the client. For a website, it's the same. Your browser - it acts as a client - will send a request to a server - and more exactly a web server - that will respond after processing.

The Web Server and PHP Interpreter - A Love Story?

As we said before, for PHP to live, it needs its interpreter. Since a Web server is not a PHP interpreter, these two elements must come into contact at a given moment. But no, unfortunately for our two friends, it's not really a relationship they love, it would be a relationship master-slave, the slave being the poor interpreter. In fact, the web server can handle different requests. For example, you can ask for an image, a static web page- that is to say, containing, for example, only XHTML and CSS - a dynamic web page - containing PHP, Python, etc. -a PDF document and many other things. When you ask him what interests us, a web page containing PHP, the web server will know it; he will determine the type of content requested from the query. When the webserver receives a request involving PHP, it will call the interpreter giving it the file to interpret and wait for the response to be sent to the client.

From these interactions, we can deduce something important: PHP runs on the server-side, it works only when the server has to respond to the request, and never when the server has already responded to the request. If you want to display a clock on your website, a clock that would update every second, would it be possible with PHP? No, because the clock would be visible to the visitor - the user of the Web browser - that when the server has already sent the response, PHP could no longer intervene. To achieve this, and more generally, for all interactions between the visitor and a web page already sent to it, we will go through another language, Javascript.

After this little overview of what PHP is, how the Web works, and the interaction between the web server and the PHP interpreter, let's move on to what we need to work. That each of you has a dedicated server in Antarctica is a bit utopian, so we will install the web server and PHP on your computer. Yes, it works, do not worry.

As a web server, we will choose the most popular and currently known: Apache HTTP Server or Apache HTTPD. This web server is published by the eponymous nonprofit organization, the Apache Software Foundation. This organization is also known for other projects as well as for their license, the Apache license, which is free and open source. But before proceeding with the installation of this software, take the time to get acquainted with the programming.

What is Programming?

Programming, sometimes described as mystical, sometimes described as incredibly complicated, what is it really? For me, programming is every day. Not because I have a nose stuck to my PC eight hours a day, but because of programming, you do it every day. Let's take an example that should speak to everyone: driving a car. With a car, you can do some basic operations, including:

To brake, to advance and to turn. There are other operations, but these will suffice for the example. Well happy in your car, you arrive at work, school or elsewhere if you wish, in any case, the time to park has arrived.

Here you are facing a problem, how to fit nicely in this location? Solve a problem, find a solution, it's programming. And solve this kind of problem, you do it every day consciously or not. That's why I like to say that programming is our everyday life. To solve this problem, what do we have at our disposal? To tell the truth, not much, but it is amply enough. We have some basic operations that allow us to move, and we also have some information on the problem, the main one being that we have room to park. All is, therefore, to manage to use, to manipulate our few operations to solve the problem. The goal is not to make you aces driving; here are the steps of the solution:

1. we advance to the height of the car than brakes;
2. we turn the wheels to the left;
3. we move in reverse, that is to say, we go back;
4. when we form a beautiful angle, we put the wheels to the right;
5. And finally, we brake at the right time to complete the maneuver.

What we have done here is to describe, to state, to express the solution to our problem, and here we are at the heart of what programming is. Our car offers us certain concepts such as the acceleration of the car or its change of direction and allows us to use these concepts through basic operations such as advance or turn, which allows us to express a solution to a problem. These few operations may not look like anything, but they are enough to express a lot of maneuvers that you could be made with a car. Once the solution is expressed, it remains only to implement it using the pedals, wheels, and other tools specific to your car.

A computer language, like PHP, for example, does exactly the same thing as this car: it offers us certain concepts allowing us to express solutions as well as tools to translate these solutions into code that the interpreter can execute. It must be understood that programming is not just one thing but two distinct steps: solving the problem and applying the solution. The solution to the problem is the design of the program, whereas the application of the solution is its implementation, the translation into code. We will come back later on the design and implementation; the important thing is that you remember that the programming takes place in two stages.

Attitude to Adopt When You Want to Learn

If you decide to continue this course - and I hope you will be many in this case - what attitude to adopt? As my introduction implied, I'm not here to make fast food version programming. My goal is not to make you learn the realms of PHP. So you will sometimes have to be a little patient before seeing the fruit of your efforts.

As for my explanations, I will not take you for morons. Although we are debuting, we are not babies; we can think and to fend for ourselves. That's why I'll often get you started with an "RTFM" - Read The Fucking Manual - or the trickier version: look for yourself. I do not want to make you assisted. I will help you, I will guide you, but I will not give you everything cooked in the bottom of the beak. You will be, without any doubt, forced at one time or another to look for yourself. This ability, this resourcefulness is a very important quality, so I want you to use it, and for this, I obviously do not have to make your professional assistantship. Of course, it will sometimes happen that even looking for a time, you cannot find a solution. In this case, you will have to ask for help on the forums of the site of zero, for example. If you do, or rather, when you do, do not forget some things.

The Title of the Subject

Let's say I have a problem, and my search did not help. I go to a forum about PHP, and I create a new topic. The first thing you need to pay attention to is the title. It aims to describe your subject; thus, people visiting the forum will know if they are likely to help you without having to read the message. It is, therefore, imperative to choose a title that describes your subject. If you put something like "Big problem," "Need urgent help," etc., you do not know what the topic is.

Small rather amusing detail, some people put a title of the style "Problem with PHP." We cannot say that it does not describe the subject, but do not you find it logical that in a forum devoted to PHP, we speak of ... PHP? It's just to say that you do not need to specify that you're talking about PHP.

We saw what not to do, but how to choose a good title, finally?

Well, there is no magic method; you have to think. If I have a problem wanting to display a text, what could I put as a title? If I put the "PHP problem," it is useless. By cons, a title like "Problem to display a text" is already more explicit, right?

You must try to summarize the purpose of the subject in a few words. If you do that, you will often have a good title. If you cannot summarize your topic, simply put the keywords that you think are most relevant.

The Content Of The Subject

After the title comes the content of the subject. The title is the summary; the content is the body of the subject. The first thing one must see in your subject is a polite phrase. Yes, when I do not see "Hello" or anything else, I do not like it, and I do not answer the subject. Politeness holds in a few words, a few seconds of your time, but many people neglect it. If I come to your house to ask for sugar this way: "Give me some sugar," are you going to give me some? I think not.

Now, if I say, "Hello, could you lend me some sugar? Thank you very much, "I already have a better chance of finishing my cake. It's the same thing when you make a topic in a forum. A touch of politeness will ensure a warmer welcome from those who help you. You have to make sentences that make sense, you must pay attention to your spelling (no SMS), and you must express yourself clearly.

Sometimes people write their subject so badly that we do not understand anything on demand. And in this kind of case, it's kind of hard to help. If you need to put PHP or other code in your subject, pay attention too! Indeed, some forums provide tools to make the reading of it more enjoyable, and it is easier to provide help when the code is more readable.

Second important thing: do not put a pie of code

Sometimes people have a little problem, but lazy to look a little where it comes from: they put us hundreds of lines of code. Do you think we'll read them? If so, you dream.

Forum visitors will not spend two hours trying to figure out where the mistake came from and five minutes to answer you. That's why you have to extract the parts of your code that are responsible for the error. For the moment, you do not know how to do it, but PHP is well designed, and it is relatively easy to find where the errors come from, we'll see that later.

Respect

Last thing that matters to me: respect for those who help you. These people use their free time to help you, so respect them. We do not ask to bend, but a simple "thank you" when the problem is solved is so much fun. Also, do not wait for the solution to be served on a silver platter. Ideally, those who help you will only point out the cause of the error, they will give you tips to correct it, but it's up to you to correct yourself. Do not come back five minutes later because you do not understand what they are saying to you. Seek for yourselves what they are pointing out to you; otherwise, you will never be able to get by on their own.

Now that you know that a web server is needed to get a web page, that the PHP needs to be interpreted by the PHP interpreter, and that you have an idea of the interactions between the web server and the PHP interpreter, you are almost dressed. Hurry to read the next chapter to complete your preformation; you will be ready to attack the learning of PHP itself!

The Programmer's Toolbox

In this chapter, we will talk about installing the tools you will need to do PHP: we will equip your machine to make it a web server capable of processing PHP. And for that we need to install some tools, hence this chapter. You already know two of these tools: PHP obviously and the Apache webserver. There is, however, a tool missing to have a perfect set: the code editor.

The surprise guest: the code editor

Before embarking on the installation of Apache and PHP, let's introduce the surprising tool: a good code editor. Well, let's be clear; this choice does not matter much right now. Since we are starting out, we will not really do a "project," everything we do will be limited to one or two PHP files. To release a heavy editor is, therefore, useless for the moment. That's why currently, at the level of the code editor, the choice does not matter. The only really essential function at our level is syntax highlighting.

It is a tool; this coloring is a very basic tool, but oh so useful, it is almost the incarnation of Chuck Norris. Small example:

```
Code: PHP
<?php
$toChar = function() use($collation) {
return $collation += 42;
};
Code: Console
<?php
```

```
$toChar = function() use($collation) { return
$collation += 42;
};
```

These codes are useless and are ugly but illustrate the contribution of syntax highlighting: greater legibility of the code. By coloring the different elements of the language in different colors, it is easier to navigate. Another advantage sometimes more difficult to perceive of this coloring is its tendency to make us discover errors in code, example:

```
Code: Console
<? Php
$ string = 'Hello, there was the old troll here,
where is he?';
Code: PHP
<? Php
$ string = 'Hello, there was the old troll here,
where is he?';
```

These two codes present a syntax error, and if it passes relatively unnoticed without syntax highlighting, it is almost impossible to miss with.

Windows

For this system, I recommend notepad ++, which you have an illustration in Figure 2.1. This program is pretty light and easy to handle, but still has a lot of tools that will make your life easier. I only use it occasionally, but I often turn to him when I have to edit a small PHP code.

Under Gnu / Linux

If you are keen on the console, Vim and Emacs will offer you syntax highlighting and countless tools. These tools are so powerful that it is difficult to understand them completely, but if it is just a matter of having some syntax highlighting, it is not very complex.

On Mac Osx And Others

Having no Mac and never really touching other systems than Windows and GNU / Linux, I am unfortunately unable to help you with these systems. If you have good little code editors easy to handle for these systems, thank you for letting me know, I will integrate them immediately!

About Encoding

Before going any further, make sure your text editor uses UTF-8 encoding without BOM by default. This setting is often found in the preferences of your code editor. Under notepad ++ for example, you must go to the "Settings" tab, click on "Preferences" and go to the "New document/folder" tab of the window that has just opened. You can then choose UTF-8 without BOM as encoding. We will see later why this is important. If you cannot find UTF-8 without BOM, just put UTF-8.

Now that we are equipped for code editing so let's move on to installing Apache and PHP!

Apache And Php On Windows

You must have administrative rights on your machine to proceed with the installation.

Go to the Apache HTTPD site, where you will find a "from a mirror" link in the left menu next to "download." Currently, the page on which you arrive offers four releases:

- 2.3.8-alpha,
- 2.2.16,
- 2.0.63,
- 1.3.42.

This can obviously evolve, just take the most recent version that is neither alpha nor beta. In my case, I will take the release 2.2.16. You then have the choice between various options such as Unix Source, Win32 Source, or Win32 Binary. Since you are on Windows, take one of the Win32 Binary, the Win32 Binary including OpenSSL. Once the file is downloaded, run it.

At the beginning of the installation, you will be asked to accept the license, so do that once you have arrived at the domain selection screen and some other information.

Then, you will have a choice between two types of installation: Typical and Custom. Since we are not here to learn how to set up a Web server with little onions, we will choose the Typical option. The actual installation will now begin, it should not take very long, a few minutes at most. Once this is complete, the installation wizard will take leave; you will have to look in the Windows taskbar. You should have a tiny, cute little icon.

Now open your favorite browser and go to http://localhost.com. The text could possibly vary; the important thing is that you do not have an error saying that the host does not exist, that it is unreachable, or I do not know what.

What Is "Local Host"?

Remember that Apache is a web server. To contact him, we must, therefore, go through the Web and, more precisely, by a web address, a URL. In the same way that the URL http://siteduzero.com puts you in contact with the webserver of the site of the zero, http://localhost puts us in contact with the Web server, which is installed on your machine. If by chance it does not work, do not panic, we will try to fix it. To do so, we will have to go to the Windows Service Manager. Press the Windows and R keys simultaneously; this will open the window. Enter the value "services.msc" and validate, then you will discover the service manager.

In the list of services, you should find the Apache HTTPD service. If it is not there, the installation did not proceed correctly, or you did not install Apache HTTPD as a service. In both cases, try to reinstall the server. If you find it and it is not in the "Started" state, right-click on it, and you can start it.

PHP's Turn

PHP is no more complicated to install than Apache, so start by going to the PHP for Windows download page. You will find various versions of PHP, take the most recent. For my part, it will be PHP 5.3.3. Among the four solutions proposed for your version of PHP, look for the "VC9 x86 Thread Safe" and download the "install." Once this download is complete, run the freshly acquired file. Just like Apache, you will be asked to accept the license, so do that, check the box "Apache 2.2.x Module", it will allow your webserver to use the PHP interpreter.

Then continue the installation, you will quickly be on a screen inviting you to choose the path to the configuration Apache - Select Apache Configuration Directory. Click on the "browse" button to choose the folder, by default, it is located in C: \ Program Files \ Apache Software Foundation \ Apache (version) \. All you have to do is select the conf folder and confirm.

While the screens continue to scroll, stop at the one titled "Choose items to install." In this screen, you can see which PHP components will install. Pull down the "extension" menu and activate Multibyte String and PostgreSQL if it is not already done. Then pull down the "PDO" menu and activate the PostgreSQL there. You just have to validate all that, the installation will then be done. Congratulations, everything should be installed. To check this, go to the Apache installation folder you chose earlier and create a test.php file in the htdocs folder. Do not forget to use your favorite code editor, put the following content in it, and save:

It's time to restart your browser and enter the following address: http://localhost/test.php.

Only one detail remains to be fixed for your installation to be ready to serve. Currently, you will see if you restart your PC or change users, Apache starts automatically. I guess like me, you have a life, so you do not spend all your time doing PHP, so it's useless for Apache to be running all the time. To avoid this, there are two things to do.

To get started, return to the Windows Service Manager as explained above and find the Apache line. Right-click on it and click on "Property," the window of Figure 2.13 will open. From this window, you can change Apache's startup mode from "Automatic" to "Manual."

Changing the Startup Mode of Apache

Thanks to this, Apache will not start any more by itself; you will have to start it yourself. However, you will notice that the icon in the taskbar persists. This is not mysterious, it is simply that this icon does not represent the server but an application that allows you to stop, start, and restart the server. Let's prevent its automatic execution. To do so, press the Windows and R keys again, but this time enter the value "MSConfig." Once validated, a new window will open, click on the "Start" tab. You find in the list just below a line referring to Apache, uncheck it, click on "Apply," and finally "Ok." Windows will prompt you to restart the system; it is not necessary to do it.

Prevent Starting The Monitor Apache Servers Application

Apache is now definitely calm and it will not bother you if you do not ask. To start Apache, two solutions are available to you. You know the first, just go through the service manager. The second involves the command prompt, which is in the list of installed programs. In this prompt, you only need to enter the net start apache2.2 command to start Apache, as shown in Figure 2.15. You may need to enter something other than apache2.2. You will find the exact name of the service in the service manager. To stop the service, nothing very complicated, it will be enough to use the command net stop instead of net start.

Apache and PHP under GNU / Linux, Mac OS X, and others.

You must have administrative rights on your machine to proceed with the installation.

GNU / Linux installation

For example, I chose a fairly popular distribution right now: The installation procedure should have little or no variation depending on your distribution; use your favorite package manager, and everything should be fine. If you still have difficulties, please refer to the documentation of your distribution or to forums of mutual help. You can also send me some oddities or problems related to a particular distribution, I will report them in this course. Just like on Windows, the first thing to do is to install the Apache server. Nothing special, the apache2 package is there for that:

We will immediately check that Apache is installed, started and functional:

```bash
Code: Bash
$ service apache2 status
# should show Apache is running (pid xyz)
```

```bash
# if it is not, make a sudo service apache2 start to
start Apache
$ wget http: // localhost
$ more index.html
# should show <html><body><h1> it works ...
```

What is the "localhost"?

Remember that Apache is a web server. To contact him, we must, therefore, go through the Web and, more precisely, by a web address, a URL. In the same way that the URL http://siteduzero.com puts you in contact with the webserver of the site of the zero, http://localhost puts us in contact with the Web server, which is installed on your machine.

Before installing PHP, you will have to check the version of it. Indeed, the necessary version, 5.3, is relatively recent, so it is possible that for some distributions, the package provided is not suitable. Let's check this:

```
Code: Bash
$ sudo apt-cache show php5
# The version part should give the value 5.3 or
higher
```

If the PHP version is correct, perfect, install the package. If, unfortunately, it is not the case, two solutions open to you. The first is to find out if a nice contributor has not created a repository or package specifically to PHP 5.3 or above, in which case you just have to change the repository or download the package directly. If you do not find any suitable repository or package, the second solution will be to compile PHP.

Let's start by retrieving the source code found it at this address. In the latest version, the source code is provided compressed with Bzip2 or Gzip, take what you prefer, I chose the Gzip. All that remains is to move the archiver, extract it, configure the installation, and finally proceed with the installation.

```bash
Code: Bash
$ sudocp /home/cedric/Downloads/php-5.3.3.tar.gz
/ Usr / local / src
$ cd / usr / local / src
$ sudo tar -xvzf php-5.3.3.tar.gz
$ cd php-5.3.3.tar.gz
$ ./configure --with-apxs2 = / usr / bin / apxs2 --
with-gettext --enable- mbstring --with-pdo-pgsql --
with-pgsql
$ sudo make
$ sudo make install
```

If during the installation, you encounter an error because of apxs2 or libxml2, you will probably need to install two additional packages:

```bash
Code: Bash
# the package to install if you have a problem with
apxs2
$ sudo apt-get install apache2-threaded-dev
# the package to install if you have a problem with
libxml2
$ sudo apt-get install libxml2-dev
```

If you still have a problem with apxs2, maybe the path is incorrect. In this case, simply replace

/usr/bin/apxs2 by the path to apxs2, you should find it easily.

Once PHP is installed, it remains to test that. But before, do not forget to restart the Apache server via a $ sudo service apache2 restart. To proceed with the test, we will create a PHP file called test.php. For my part, I have to create this file in the folder/var/ www. If this is not the case for you, look for the httpd.conf file located in the conf folder of the Apache installation folder, there you will find a line defining the "DocumentRoot," it is the folder in question. In this file, place the following content:

```
Code: PHP
<? phpphpinfo ();
```

We can now check that it works:

```
Code: Bash
$ wget http: //localhost/test.php
$ cat test.php | grep 'PHP Version'
# should show <a href="http://www.php.net/"> ... <h1
class = "p"> PHP Version 5.3.2-1ubuntu4.2 </ h1>
```

Just like Windows, it can be interesting to control when Apache starts. I'll let you refer to your distribution's documentation to prevent the service from starting. To start or stop Apache, you will just have to use the service command with a start or stop arguments. The installation is now complete. Congratulations!

Chapter Two

Configure To Better Rule

Before using our freshly installed tools, it is necessary to configure them. I reassure you right that we are not going to configure the little onions PHP and Apache. But still, some things have to be done.

PHP Configuration

The configuration of PHP is centralized in a file, the famous php.ini. It's a pretty simple file that matches the keys to values. There is, for example, a key for default identifiers for connections and the values associated with these identifiers. What we will do next is to configure PHP so that it can be used in good conditions for learning. The first thing to do is to locate the configuration file. This step is relatively easy; the answer is in the previous lines, in the test file we created. Go back to your favorite browser and go to http: //localhost/test.php. In the page received, do a search for "Loaded Configuration File," you will have the path to the configuration file next to it.

Open this file and look for three lines starting with: error_reporting,display_errors, and date.timezone.

On each of these lines, you find the principle of key and value, the syntax being <key> = <value>. We will change the value of these three keys. Put this as a value:

```ini
Code: Ini
error_reporting = E_ALL | E_STRICT display_errors =
On
date.timezone = 'Europe / Brussels'
```

It should be noted that for the last key, the value depends on your geographical position. You can find the most suitable value on this page of the PHP documentation. For example, I live in Europe, so I click on the corresponding link and the nearest city to my place of residence in Brussels, so I take the value Europe / Brussels, all surrounded by apostrophes.

I will, of course, explain to you later why we did that.

Apache Configuration

Like PHP, Apache is configured using a file, the httpd.conf. This file is located in the conf folder of the Apache installation folder. The syntax is not the same as that of php.ini, but it is not more complicated. Open this httpd.conf and look for the line defining the DocumentRoot. This DocumentRoot is the location where Apache will fetch the files that are requested. Let's take an example: if I go to http: //localhost/test.php, I contact the webserver at http: // localhost and ask for the file test.php. This file, where will Apache go to get it? In the DocumentRoot. You can test it: delete or rename the test.php file that you created after installing Apache, and you will find that the URL http: //localhost/test.php leads you to an error.

Depending on your operating system - typically Windows - the DocumentRoot may be in a folder that requires administrator privileges, you would still need to be an administrator whenever you want to create a new file or modify a new one. To avoid this, we will modify this DocumentRoot. On the machine where I am, the DocumentRoot is C: \ Program Files \ Apache Software_Foundation \ Apache2.2 \ htdocs, I'm going to change to C: \ www for example, it does not really matter as long as it's a folder where you can create and edit files. Remain the last modification to perform, look in the file line <Directory "DocumentRoot">. Of course, remember to replace DocumentRoot with the old value, so in my case, I have to look for <Directory "C: \ Program Files \ Apache Software Foundation \ Apache2.2 \ htdocs">. In this line, we will change the path since we changed the DocumentRoot.

In summary, at the beginning we had, for example, this:

```
Code: Apache
DocumentRoot "C: \ Program Files \ Apache Software
Foundation \ Apache2.2 \ htdocs"
<Directory "C: \ Program Files \ Apache Software
Foundation \ Apache2.2 \ htdocs">
And in the end, we have for example this:
Code: Apache
DocumentRoot "C: \ www"
<Directory "C: \ www">
```

When you modify the Apache configuration file, it must be reloaded for the changes to take effect. Remember to do this reload if your system allows or failing to restart Apache completely.

Well, here you go, you've installed your own web server and PHP, not to mention a code editor. You have everything you need and you are ready to attack PHP learning. One day maybe someone will tell you that you are crazy to have installed this software this way. Indeed, you should know that ready-made packs exist, packs that install PHP, Apache and other software alone as big. If I chose not to use these packs, it's because none of them contained all the software I needed in the right version and then because I think it's good to have a small idea of how we install - even fairly basic - this different software.

First steps

After these long minutes spent installing, testing, and configuring different software, I feel you want to start the real learning. That's why without waiting, I suggest you to see what are the PHP tags and comments and what is their usefulness.

PHP tags

Let's take a PHP file, very cute, very small, very soft, that of the previous chapter:

```
Code: PHP - Example 1
<? phpphpinfo ();
```

I will rewrite it in another form, which it will be simpler for my explanation:

```
Code: PHP - Example 2
<? phpphpinfo ();
?>
```

As we have seen, PHP is an interpreted language; the interpreter will read this file and process it. Small problem: a PHP file can contain PHP but can also contain other things, text, HTML, CSS, Javascript and I do not know what else. This is a perfectly valid PHP file content:

```
Code: PHP - Example 3
Hello, Robert.
<? phpphpinfo ();
?>
Goodbye, Paul, the fisherman.
```

Of course, the PHP interpreter does not understand these texts; they do not mean anything to it since it is not a legal PHP syntax. One says of a code, a syntax, that it is licit if it respects the grammar and the syntax of the language. Worse, if the interpreter tried to do something with this text, it would send you a nice mistake, so your PHP code would be useless. This is why PHP tags are so important; they will tell the interpreter what PHP code is and so it must treat and what is not. If you want to signal the beginning of a PHP code, you will have to indicate it to him via the opening tag - <? Php - whereas if you want to signal him the end of a PHP code, you will use the closing tag -?>. As you may have noticed, the code in the previous chapter does not have a closing tag, but it still works. The behavior of the interpreter is therefore very simple: "When I meet the opening tag, I start processing the code until I meet the closing tag, or have read all the code." In this regard, I recommend you not to put a closing tag, unless it is necessary, as in example 3. Some things are incomprehensible to the interpreter before and after the PHP code, so it is necessary to put both tags. This recommendation will be explained to you later.

During your learning, your PHPiens course, you met these pairs of tags:

```
<? and?>,
<? = and?> and
<script language = "php"> and </ script>.
```

These pairs of tags have been or are still, unfortunately, lawful. But eventually, they will not be, so you should not use them. These are old practices prone to separation that may already be unusable depending on the configuration of PHP. Among the examples above, you now know the role of each item besides this one: phpinfo ();. We will see what it is later, promised.

For fun, I propose a mini TP: write me a legitimate PHP content with elements that are not PHP.

Code: PHP

```
<? phpphpinfo ();
?>
```

I bet you broke your head looking for something complicated ...

```
<? phpphpinfo ();
?>
```

while it's really stupid. :)

```
<? Php
phpinfo ();
```

Anything that is not PHP is excluded from opening and closing tags, so it's legal PHP content.

Comments

Now that you know the tags that are used to delimit the PHP code, we'll see another very important element

: comments.

Like all languages, PHP allows commenting, that is, elements between PHP tags that will not be interpreted. As it may not be clear, we will use the example code from the previous chapter and make a small change:

```
Code: PHP - Example 4
<? Php
// phpinfo ();
```

Put that in your test.php file and go to the address you now know well, what happens before your eyes amazed? In a word: nothing. Yes, I sneaked a comment in this code, the phpinfo () element has not been interpreted, and since it was he who was at the origin of this charming painting, it remains only the empty.

So you guessed it: the PHP interpreter considers everything following two slashes (//) as a comment. The PHP interpreter does not interpret what is commented on, he ignores it.

What interest, then?

For the interpreter, there is none; it does not care about your comments. But for you, developers, comments are vital. For the moment, your scripts are ridiculously simple and tiny. But later, when you start doing much longer and more complex scripts, the comments will become essential so that you, or someone else, can find you in the code. Imagine that you make a very long code, very complex and involving many elements. A few months later, for one reason or another, you have to change it. If you have not commented, you will have trouble finding your marks, and you will lose time. You might not even understand anything at all.

But be careful, do not fall into the opposite excess. Indeed, we sometimes see scripts in which each line is commented. Eventually, it's possible to find that pretty, but it's not the purpose of the comments, they are not made to translate your script into another language!

They are here to help you find your code. If you start putting a comment to say that you make an addition, it is no longer useful. So you must be careful not to abuse it, use it sparingly when you need to point out something more general. If, for example, you use Mr. Patate's method, it is very useful to put a little comment saying that the following code is an implementation of Mr. Patate's method.

Let's go back to the previous code and modify it again:

```
Code: PHP - Example 5
<? Php
// phpinfo ();
phpinfo ();
```

What Do You Think Will Happen?

Are we going to see the big picture twice? Once ? Or will we see nothing at all? The answer is: we'll see the big picture once.

Why? The answer is simple. I said that // was used to indicate a comment. Only the comment is "effective" only on the line where the // are.

The first phpinfo (); is therefore ignored because it follows //, but as the second is on another line, it is not a comment, and it generates a large table.

You can have fun putting the second phpinfo (); on the same line as the first, both will be comments, and you will see a blank page.

So you know how to comment a line, but imagine that you wanted to comment on several. I take the previous code, and I want to put both phpinfo (); in a comment but leaving them on two different lines.

The code will look like this:

```
Code: PHP - Example 6
<? Php
// phpinfo ();
// phpinfo ();
```

But you will agree: if we have many lines to comment, it will quickly become heavy to put //; if for some reason you want to comment or uncomment a large block of code, you would lose a lot of time typing or erasing all //.

That's why there is a second method for commenting on text. Better than a long speech: a piece of code.

```
Code: PHP - Example 7
<? Php
/ * phpinfo (); phpinfo ();
* /
```

Test this code. What is going on ? Again, you find yourself facing a blank page.

As you will have understood: everything between / * and * / is considered as a comment. Attention, however! The comment begins at the first / * and ends at first * /.

Again, a piece of code:

```
Code: PHP - Example 8
 <? Php
/ *
/ * phpinfo ();
* /
phpinfo ();
* /
```

If you test this code, you will see something new and unexpected: a PHP error!

If you understand that the comment starts on the first / * and ends on the first * /, you should be able to explain why.

When the PHP interpreter interprets your code, it finds a / * and says: "A comment starts, I do not know anything until I find a * /"; he continues to read your code and meets this famous * /. Just after that, it reads phpinfo ();, which is a valid statement: no problem, the read continues. Now he comes to the last line, the one that contains the second * /. You know that it indicates the end of a comment on several lines, only the interpreter did not find an opening for this comment multi-lines. He finds himself in front of a text he has to interpret, only * / means nothing to him.

The interpreter, therefore, returns an error stating that it does not understand your script and finishes it. If you use a text editor with syntax highlighting, as I advised you in the previous chapter, you should never make a comment error. Indeed, they stand out from the rest of the code by a color or a different writing font (as you have seen in the codes I gave you).

Here you are unbeatable on comments in PHP, so make me very useful and relevant!

This too much chapter, unfortunately, ends already, but do not neglect its importance. As I told you, and as I will tell you again, it is by having a solid knowledge of the basics that you will be able to build great things. Anyway, do not worry, if you like the chapters more consequent, I bet that the next will make you vibrate like the rope of a bow coming to uncheck an arrow!

Chapter Three

Variables, The Heart Of PHP

We will tackle a fundamental chapter. You're going to have to hang on because it's going to go very fast. You will be confronted with one of the longest chapters and you will see many new things, so do not go too fast. Take your time, and of course, do not hesitate to re-read several times if necessary!

First Approach

A variable ... But What is It?

In mathematics, a variable is a name, a symbol representing an unknown quantity or whatever belonging to a given domain.

In computing, it's about the same: a variable associates a name with a value that can change over time. We will take an example. Imagine that you have a bag full of apples. The bag is the name of the variable, and the apples contained in the bag are the value of the variable. I can easily replace the apples that are in the bag with pears, for example. The name of the variable is always the same (the bag), but the value of the variable has changed: instead of apples, we have pears.

Variables represent a fundamental concept of any programming language. That's why I called this part "Variables, the heart of PHP." You will shuffle variables when you do PHP (or any other programming language). For now, you know that their names and value characterize variables. Only, there is a third characteristic that is of paramount importance: the type of value.

Take the example of the bag filled with apples. The bag is the name of the variable, the apples are the value of the variable, but what is the type of this value? It's simple; apples are fruit. The variable is therefore of the "fruit" type. Now, if I put steaks in my bag, the name of the variable remains the same, the value changes, but the type also changes! Indeed, a steak is meat: the variable is then of the "meat" type.

If I had replaced apples with pears, the value of the variable would have changed, but not the type! Yes, pears are also fruits. You can see that the type of the variable always matches the type of the value: both must match.

The only purpose of this tirade on apricots is to introduce the concept of variable, name, value, and type. If you do not understand this concept, do not go further, read again and try to understand again.

Variables With PHP Sauce

Nice, we understood the concept of variable. Only, I must admit something: each programming language has special rules for variables. Of course, here I will talk about variables with PHP.

Better than a long speech, we will create our first variable in PHP! Type this code, save it in a PHP file, open this file, and open your eyes!

```
Code: PHP
<? Php
$ My_variable;
```

Congratulations, you have just created your first variable. But you still find yourself in front of a blank page; it's perfectly normal. We created a variable, we declared it, but we do nothing with it.

We will analyze together the line of code, new to you, $ ma_variable. The first symbol is a $ and is used to tell the PHP interpreter that it is a variable. When you manipulate a variable in PHP, you must always precede the name of the variable with a $. After this first symbol, you have the name of the variable itself. Here, the name of the variable is ma_variable. Be careful though! You cannot name your variables no matter how. Here is the naming rule for variables in PHP: you can use any alphabetic character (lowercase and uppercase letters included) or numeric characters, or an underscore. However, the name of the variable cannot start with a number.

Here are some examples of valid names:

- $ variable;
- $ VARIABLE;
- $ variable2;
- $ variable_3;

$ _Variable.

And now, invalid names:

- $ 1truc;
- $ answer;
- $ Var ^.

In the list of valid variable names, you can find $ variable and $ VARIABLE. You should know that in PHP, variable names are case-sensitive, which means that the PHP interpreter differentiates between lowercase and uppercase letters. And therefore, this code creates two distinct variables that can be given different values:

```
K;k
Code: PHP
 <? Php
$ Variable;
$ VARIABLE;
```

In this code, as in all others, you may notice a symbol other than the $ that comes up very often: the semicolon (;). This symbol is also very important. It is used to tell the PHP interpreter that the instruction is complete. You must put a semicolon at the end of each statement. Otherwise, the PHP interpreter will tell you that there is an error in your script.

But what is an instruction? An instruction is a piece of text that represents a lawful order for the interpreter. phpinfo (); for example is an instruction.

Do you remember the first codes? They looked like this:

```
Code: PHP
 <? phpphpinfo ();
```

What do we find? The famous semicolon marks the end of an instruction. Here, the instruction is phpinfo (), it gives the order to the interpreter to create this big table that you know so well now.

Let's go back to our variables. So far, we've seen how to create a variable (we can also call it declaring a variable). Wonderful. If I remember correctly, I bothered you with two other notions: the value and the type of a variable. So far, these two notions have not intervened. We just declared a variable without giving it any value or type. But do not look at me with sad eyes, we'll see that in a moment. Besides, you should take a break because we're going to complicate things a little bit.

Values and Assignment Operator

I told you before that you just declared a variable: in theory, it's true; in practice, it's not. Indeed, the PHP interpreter is lazy and you will see it through several things. So we declare our variable, but we do not value it. It contains nothing and is therefore useless. I do not know about you, but when I have something useless, I put it aside or get rid of it, but I certainly do not let it sit in the middle of my living room. In PHP, it's the same: your variable is not taken into account, it is not really declared, it does not exist. For it to exist, we must do something about it; we must give it a value. In our story of bag, apples, steaks and pears, giving value means filling the bag with something.

Roughly, we can say that it's the same thing in PHP. Unfortunately, I do not see myself going to open my computer to fill it. That's why PHP developers have created a very useful tool: the assignment operator (=).

A little code ... it was a long time:

```php
Code: PHP
<? Php
my_variable = VALUE;
```

Do not try to test this code or you'll get a nice mistake. As usual, let's analyze this code. In the line that interests us, we find a familiar element, a variable. Directly to his right, a new symbol and what represents a value. This new symbol, this assignment operator (=), allows us to give, to assign a value to a variable. If the variable did not exist before, that is, if we had never assigned a value before, then the PHP interpreter declares it before making the assignment.

The assignment operator is an equal (=); however, write $ my_variable = value; it does not mean that $ my_variable is equal to value. This piece of code means that we assign (or we attribute) the value of the right operand to the variable$ My_variable. It's a question of terminology, but it's important to know it!

After the name, we just saw how to give a value to a variable. Now, I tell myself that you must be impatient to hear about the guys; hang onto your belts!

A Typing Story

Name and value; now, we are going to play with the third notion: the type. But yet, this type of story is even more complex than it seems. As I said before, every language has its own rules for variables. This is true for variable names, and so is the type of variable. We can classify the programming languages according to the strength, the level of their typing. There are strongly typed languages and other weakly. A strict rule does not govern this notion of strongly or weakly typed language. But in the case of PHP, many people agree that it is weakly typed. When you do your PHP code, you do not have to worry about the type of your variables. The PHP interpreter handles this itself and changes the type on the fly if necessary.

As I am sure I have confused you, I will tell you a new story.

I go to the farmer's house and ask him to give me 3 kilos of butter and 24 eggs. Can I add up both? Does it make sense to add eggs and butter?

Well, no, it does not make sense.

On the other hand, if I now add the price of these two goods, does that make sense? Is it possible to add 4 and 6 euros? Yes, because it's the same thing: euros plus euros give euros.

You cannot manipulate different things at once. You cannot add a number and a sentence; you can add two fractions. But in PHP, you do not have to worry about that. Imagine that we have two variables: one contains a number and the other contains something else, a string, the first name "Eve," for example. If I wanted to sum these two variables in a strongly typed language, I would have problems. In PHP, no problem, you can do it. The PHP interpreter will take care of giving the right type to your variables so that the addition can be done. This operation, changing the type of a variable, is called cast or cast.

And you know what? It's the same for the assignment operator! If I type this:

```php
Code: PHP
<? Php
$ ma_variable = 5;
```

I declare a variable that has my_variable for a name, which is of type int (for integer) and of value 5. Another example:

```php
Code: PHP
<? Php
$ other_variable = 'Eve';
```

This time, I declare a variable that has other_variable for name, which is of type string (string) and value "Eve" You did not care about the type of your variables. Depending on the value you wanted to assign to a particular variable, the PHP interpreter gave the correct type to the correct variable. If you followed what I said, you should now say something like, "Uh, are you stupid? You talk to us about something totally useless or you try to confuse us for nothing or what ?! "

I admit it: the typing is not a priori something important in PHP. And yet, it will be extremely useful afterward. In fact, I lie a little (but really very little, it is more of a dead-end on detail than anything else). I tell you that a variable is of type x or y, but to be strictly accurate, I should say that the variable inherits the type of value that is assigned to it. Remember that it is very important.

Primitive Types

After my long talk about typing, how about discovering variable types in PHP? The list is not exhaustive. I am only talking here about what I call primitive types, that is, basic types. There are five.

Integers, Aka Int (Or Integer)

You've met them before, but we're still going to talk about integers again. An integer variable always contains an integer value.

For example, we find integers 1, 565, 70, and so on. All the following variables are integers:

```
Code: PHP
<?php
$a = 5;
$b = 234;
$c = -9;
```

To declare an integer, you just have to put a $, followed by the name of the variable, an equal, and finally, the number you want to assign to the variable without forgetting at the end the eternal semicolon to go up to PHP that the instruction is finished.

The Numbers With Commas, Alias Float

Integers are cool. But that is not enough. You may need decimal numbers; the type of a variable containing a floating-point number is a float (you may also encounter duplicates: in practice, both are relatively equivalent). So who can create a float variable with the value 5.25?

Easy, you tell me? Not so sure.

When you write a decimal number, you separate the whole part of the decimal part with a comma. But lack of luck, in PHP, and in many programming languages, maybe even all, the whole part is separated from the decimal part by a dot (.).

To get the variable I was talking about, we will use this code:

```
Code: PHP
<? Php
$ d = 5.25;
```

// for those who would have written "$ d = 5,25; Do not worry, we all made this mistake one day

/ *

Did you see how useful the comments are? : p

When I told you we were going to use it (well, OK, I admit, here it is useless)

True Or False, Aka Boolean

This guy is a bit special and not very natural seen like that. Short story!

Have you ever played the game? Who is it? "? For those who do not know, it is played with two, each player chooses the photo of a character and is found in front of twenty photos. Players ask questions, in turn, to eliminate photos, and find the character chosen by the other. To eliminate them, we ask simple questions like, "Does he have long hair? Or "Is it a woman? ". To these kinds of questions, there are only two possible answers: yes or no.

To declare an integer, you just have to put a $, followed by the name of the variable, an equal, and finally, the number you want to assign to the variable without forgetting at the end the eternal semicolon to go up to PHP that the instruction is finished.

The second very important point is the name of your variables. Indeed, the name of a variable is a capital element: if it is too long, it would be annoying to type (for example, $ NombreMessagesParPage is a variable name certainly very clear, but a frightening length). You must limit yourself and do not exaggerate.

However, do not fall into the opposite excess. If you put variable names too short, you may not know what this variable is (for example, $ inf is a very short name, but it does not tell me anything at all). So you have to find a balance between clarity and length. The idea is to have a style of variables. Take the words you use most often in your variable names, and find diminutives. For example, instead of a number, you can put Nb, instead of information, put Info. You can also delete all the white words like "from," "by," etc.

If I take the example of $ NombreMessagesParPage, it will give $ nb_mess_page. It's much shorter, but it's just as legible as long as you always keep the same naming convention.

Variables, that's a funny thing, by the way. Ever wondered when it was useful to create a variable? Often, it happens that we see this kind of script:

```php
Code: PHP
<? Php
function cube ($ nb)
{
$ calculation = $ nb * $ nb * $ nb;
return $ calculation;
}
$ rating = 5;
```

```php
$ volume = cube ($ odds);
echo 'The volume of a 5cm side cube is'. $ Volume;
?>
```

Can anyone tell me how the $ calculus, $ quote, and $ volume variables are useful?

This kind of variable - I call it parasites. Any variable takes up some space in the server's memory. The more variables there are, the less memory there is, the slower the server (well, it's a bit too simplistic, but the idea is there). When you know you will not use a variable, do not create it! Often, coders are afraid of arrays at first, so we often see bits of code like these:

```php
Code: PHP
<? Php
$ max_size = $ array ['max_size'];
$ min_size = $ array ['min_size'];
$ max_width = $ array ['max_width'];
$ min_width = $ array ['min_width'];
?>
```

You may be kidding, but a lot of coders do that, and it's useless. You create totally useless variables that slow down the server. In Part II of this tutorial, we will see many more practical examples where we would be tempted to create useless variables, but for now, just remember that you have to think carefully before creating variables. Here is the previous script without unnecessary variables:

```php
Code: PHP
<? Php
function cube ($ nb)
{
return $ nb * $ nb * $ nb;
}
echo 'The volume of a 5cm side cube is'. Cube (5);
?>
```

The rendering is the same, but I saved three useless variables!

Two more details that make me climb to the ceiling when I meet them on scripts: the first concerns strings delimited by quotation marks. You know that in these strings, the variables are replaced by their value. So sometimes we get these kinds of things:

```php
Code: PHP
<? Php
$ a = any_function ();
echo "$ a";
?>
```

Who in the room can give me one good reason to put quotation marks around $ a?

It is useless, the rendering will be exactly the same if we remove them, and in addition, it will be much more powerful. Indeed, analyze the string and possibly replace a variable by its value; it takes a long time! Whereas just displaying a variable, it goes at superluminal speed.

Second detail: let's talk about concatenation. Who can tell me where is the stupidity in this script (except useless variables, it is, for example)?

```php
Code: PHP
<? Php
$ a = 5;
$ b = 6;
$ c = 11;
echo ''. $ a. '+'. $ b. '='. $ c. '';
?>
```

For those who are attentive, it is these two empty chains (") that do not have the slightest meaning. What is the point of concatenating an empty string? Let's take a real example: imagine that you stick sticks to pieces. What would it be like to stick a stick of zero sizes? Apart from wasting time sticking, it is useless at all. Well, it's the same when concatenating empty strings: PHP loses time concatenating while concatenating an empty string does not change the other string! It sounds stupid said like that, but a lot of people do this stupidity.

Chapter Four

The Bible of the PHP Coder

In this tutorial, I have already given you one or two links to you to be part of the site http://fr.php.net. But what is this site? This site is a gold mine. In theory, to become a good PHP coder (or at least, to know all the technical aspects of language), just browse this site. Only, at first sight, it seems austere and unattractive. I will explain a little how you get out.

First, when you come to this site, look in the list of links at the top. You can see Download, Documentation, Faq, etc. The link we are interested in is documentation. When you click on it, you come to a page. You can see a table on this page; there are the lines Formats, View Online and Download. What interests us is to see the online documentation (on the PHP Group website): we will look in the line View Online! It is from here that you can reach all the articles of the documentation. You can see that everything is classified by theme. Look at point III, Language Reference, for example. If you look at the names of the pages of this theme, you must recognize them. Functions, variables, expressions, control structures, we saw all this in this tutorial. There are others that we have not seen, such as references, classes, and objects, but it is not very important at the moment. What I want you to understand is that everything is classified by theme. And so, if you are looking for something in the documentation, the first thing to do is to ask what is the theme of what you are looking for.

If I want information about the if (), I know it's a control structure, so I'll see in point III: 16, the control structures. If you click on this link, you will come to a new table of contents: the table of contents of the control structures. Yes, there are many structures, so we put them all on different pages to not mix everything.

So click on the link of the yew, and you are faced with the description of its role, it's functioning, etc. You also have code examples: I invite you to test them often; it will help you understand.

If you continue down the page, you will sometimes see notes (in red, yellow) that are additions, clarifications and that you must read. It sometimes contains crucial information.

But be careful not to give a blind trust in these notes as there can be big mistakes (already seen several times). You must always criticize what you read.

Now that we have seen a little what the documentation (doc 'for intimates) was, I will show you what you will use most often: the list of functions. We learned to do functions, but there are already tons, more than a thousand! Knowing this, it is very important, before creating a function, to check that it does not already exist. But how to know?

It's very simple. Let's take a real case. We will imagine that I want to create a function that calculates the square root of a number.

The first thing to do is to ask, "What is the theme of my research?". I am looking for a function and the theme is the function. I go to the table of contents of the documentation, and I go down to the VI, the reference of the functions. I know I'm looking for a job, but what else do I know? I know that square roots are part of mathematics. So I'm going to look for the table of contents of mathematical functions. So I look in the list, and I get to point LXXIX, Mathematics. Cool, that's what I want. I click on the link, and here I am on the table of contents of mathematical functions.

Go down a little on the page, and you will see the table of contents. This table lists all the functions and gives a very brief explanation of the role of each of them. So I'm going to look for a section where we talk about square root. I'm looking for, I'm still searching, and I'm falling on the function sqrt () whose description is Square root. Great, chances are that's what I'm looking for! So I click on the link, and here I am on the page about the function sqrt ().

On this new page, you have several pieces of information. First, roughly, and in blue, you have the name of the function (here, sqrt ()). Just below, you have parentheses with a text like this, for example, PHP 4, PHP 5. It tells you for which versions of PHP this function exists. If you use a version of PHP that is not indicated between these parentheses, you will have a fatal error. You can have something more complex like: PHP 4> = 4.3.0, PHP 5. This means that the function is defined for PHP 4 version from PHP 4.3.0, and for PHP 5.

You then have a new line containing the name of the function and a short description.

But how to read that?

First, the first word, float. This is the type of value the function returns to you, here afloat, a floating-point number. Remember primitive types and arrays. You may have the word void, and if so, it means that the function does not return any value.

Then comes the name of the function, here sqrt ().

The parentheses follow, they will give you the number of parameters and the type requested. In the case of sqrt (), there is only one parameter, a floating-point number, the number of which we want to calculate the square root. For each parameter, you will have a name and a type. Some types are still unknown, such as mixed or callback. These last two types are pseudo-types; they do not really exist, it's just to simplify the reading.

Here are the three pseudo-types:

Mixed: indicates that any type can be given for the argument.

Callback: indicates that you must give the name of a callback function.

Number: indicates that we must give a number, integer or not.

For callback functions, we'll see that later, do not worry.

It is possible to see some arguments in brackets ([]). Don't be surprised, it just means that they are optional and you do not have to inform them (remember, I showed you how to create functions with optional arguments?). Once the prototype is read and understood, you come across a complete description of the function. Be sure to read it because it's very important.

In the case of the sqrt () function, there is only one parameter, and we easily guess what it is for. Only this is not the case with all functions. Take, for example, the mysql_real_escape_string () function. Look after the description - you have a new big title: List of parameters. This section will tell you what the purpose of this or that parameter is. It is very important to read this section as it is she who will let you know how to use the function.

The following section tells you about the value of return and it is also very important. Imagine the following case: I'm affecting a variable the return of a function that can return either a number or a Boolean. Then, I use this variable as a parameter for a function that asks for a number and nothing else. What would happen if, for some reason, the first function returned a Boolean? You would have an error, and the second function would crash!

Errors of this kind are very common (we will see a very good example in part II of this tutorial), so be very careful and always check the type of your variables when it is not safe (if a function can return two types and there is only one that suits you, you have to check what returns the function with an if, for example). We continue to descend and new sections: examples. As I said before, they are very useful and helpful to understand the function better so do not hesitate to try them! The rest is known, so I'm done! You now know how to find a function without knowing its name, so if you come on a forum to ask if this or that function exists, you will have no more excuse, and you will be flogged publicly.

Well, another case may come up: the one where you know the name of a function, but you do not know what it does or how it does. Often the answer to a problem is a function. The person who answers gives only the name of the function to the person who asks; it will be enough for him to solve the problem. Unfortunately, this person has not read this chapter, and she does not know how to find the function: what does she do? She posts a new message asking how the function is used. Pretty sad, right?

In five minutes, you will know how to stop having to post that kind of useless message.

The site we have been talking about for a long time has a very practical tool: a search engine. Just type the name of the function in the small form at the top right, and you will come across the description. But there is better!

You can access the description of any function via the link: http://fr.php.net/%s.

% s represents the name of the function: thus, for the function strpos (), for example, we have http://fr.php.net/strpos.

But it does not stop there: type math instead of the name of a function, boom, you come across the index pages associated with mathematical functions.

A small bonus for those who use Firefox: a handy shortcut. Start by going to the Bookmarks menu and then in the Organize bookmarks option. Then add a bookmark via the button provided for this purpose, give it the name you like, put http://en.php.net/% s as the web address, and for the keyword, write something equivocal and not too long (as doc, for example). Save it and type doc strpos in the address bar of Firefox: miracle, you come across the page that describes the function strpos (). As you've probably guessed, just change the following doc to land on the page. And you are friends with the documentation: if you follow these steps, you can always find what you are looking for!

Casting is Practical

For a few chapters already, I'm talking about something that PHP does very often: casting. It's an action that changes the type from one expression to another, and it's essential. Remember my example with the addition: who can tell me how much it is 'Apple' + 'Pear'? Well, with casting, I can answer you, it's 0!

We can cast variables in two ways: either with operators or with functions.

I will start by talking a little about the functions, the operators will follow, and the conversion table will close the way.

Three functions allow you to cast an expression to a specific type: strval (), floatval (), and intval (). Just by seeing the names of the functions, you should understand who is doing what.

strval () translates an expression into a string, for example:

```php
Code: PHP
<? Php
$ var = 5; var_dump ($ var);
$ var = strval ($ var); var_dump ($ var);
?>
```

The var_dump () we confirm, we have cast our variable! The other two functions are used in the same way:

```php
Code: PHP
<? Php
$ var = 'lala'; var_dump ($ var);
$ var = intval ($ var); var_dump ($ var);
$ var = floatval ($ var); var_dump ($ var);
?>
```

Three functions, many types, there is a problem, right?

Indeed, other types have no small function of this kind (we could create them, but it's useless). Fortunately for them, a fourth function comes to save the furniture: settype ().

This function takes two parameters: the variable that we want to cast (and not an expression, this time) and the type we want to give it.

Here is an example of its use, very simple:

```php
Code: PHP
<? Php
$ var = ''; var_dump ($ var); settype ($ var,
'int'); var_dump ($ var); settype ($ var, 'bool');
var_dump ($ var); settype ($ var, 'float'); var_dump
```

```
($ var); settype ($ var, 'array'); var_dump ($ var);
settype ($ var, 'null'); var_dump ($ var); settype
($ var, 'string'); var_dump ($ var);
?>
```

You notice that I do not affect the return value of the function to $ var: indeed, settype () works directly on the variable and not on a copy. But we'll see that later in the chapter on references.

In front of your amazed eyes, you can see the type of $ var change all over the place. Unfortunately, settype (), I do not like it. Why? Because we modify the variable directly.

Remember my example earlier, with a function that can return either a number or a boolean, and another that asks for a number and nothing else. If I want to make sure I have a number, I can either make a condition or cast my variable. Here's how we would do with settype ():

```
Code: PHP
<? Php
$ var = function_une (); settype ($ var, 'int');
echo function_two ($ var);
?>
```

Three instructions and a useless variable, rather ugly, no? Whereas with the three starting functions

```
Code: PHP
<? Php
echo function_two (intval (function_une ()));
?>
```

Shorter and sexier, what could be better?

Ben, in fact, there is better! I really do not like to use my fingers on my keyboard, and it bores me to type intval ($ var). It's time to get to know the operators!

I will take an older code and get the same result by saving my fingers:

```php
Code: PHP
<? Php
$ var = ''; var_dump ($ var); var_dump ((int) $
var); var_dump ((bool) $ var); var_dump ((float) $
var); var_dump ((array) $ var); var_dump ((string) $
var);
?>
Code: PHP
<? Php
echo function_two ((int) function_une ());
?>
```

And that's it. Now you know how to cast expressions and variables!

The priority of these operators is the same; they are all less important than the operators ++ and -, but higher priority than operators *, / and%. Do not stop in this good way: it's good to know how to cast, but it's better to know what gives the cast from one type to another.

Cast in Boolean

To start smoothly, we will cast all known types into Booleans. As you know, the boolean is either false or true. Since there is an almost infinite number of values that give true, here is what gives false when we trans type an expression into a boolean:

the boolean false; the integer 0 (zero);

the floating-point number 0.0;

the empty string '' and the strings '0' and "0"; an empty array (without any association); the NULL type.

You just have to test to make sure. Any other value than these will be true after casting to Boolean

Full Cast

If we want to convert a boolean to an integer, the integer will be 0 if the boolean is false and 1 if the boolean is true. If we want to convert a float to an integer, the integer will be worth the lower rounding if the float is positive, but if it is negative, the integer will be worth the rounding up (we round to the number closest to 0).

```php
Code: PHP
<? Php
var_dump ((int) 4.65); var_dump ((int) -4.65);
?>
```

If you want to convert a string to an integer, there are several possible cases:

if the string starts with a number ('0hello' or '3.9lala' for example), the resulting integer will be equal to the integer part of that number;

if the string does not start with a number, the resulting integer will be worth 0.

For other types (array, null, etc.), the entire cast is not defined, it can do anything. However, as it is rather nice, if you want to cast an entire array, for example, PHP will first cast the array to be boolean and then boolean to the whole.

Convert to a Floating-Point Number

If you cast a boolean to a floating-point number, two cases are possible: if the boolean is true, the float will be worth 1, otherwise 0.

If you cast a whole number to a floating-point number, the float will be worth the integer (logical, 1.0 is equivalent to 1).

If you want to cast a string to float, it's exactly like integers; it depends on where the string starts.

This number is a float: -1.3e3. This is actually another writing for (-1.3) * 10 ^ 3.

For other types, it's like with an integer.

If you convert the true boolean to a string, you get the string '1'. If the boolean is false, you get an empty string.

If you convert an integer or a decimal number, you get a string representing this number (i.e., a string which, cast to the starting type, gives the starting value).

If you try to convert an array to a string, you will get the string 'Array' (so do an echo array (), and you've just proved that PHP converts the expression into a string before displaying it).

NULL is also converted to an empty string (").

Cast in Array

This is the simplest case of all: if you cast a type to an array, you will get an array with this value as the value of the association carrying the key 0. And here we are, with casting. Strangely strong, this PHP, don't you think? This chapter was certainly long but not very complex. Don't hesitate to come and read it again as it's a good memo. And as a gift: no MCQ!

Pass Variables

After a few intensive chapters on PHP, you are slowly starting to gain some experience. Until now, you created your code, you went to the page, and you simply looked at the result without asking for more. What if we gave a little life to all this by allowing the visitor to interact with your script without modifying it?

Welcome to the magical and evil world (very important, that word) of forms and the transmission of variables.

There are several methods for passing variables, but we will start with the simplest: addresses (URLs).

For now, the URL just lets you tell your browser which files to call, but URLs hide a lot of things because they can transmit variables!

Create a PHP file, call it url.php and type this code:

```php
Code: PHP
<? Php
echo '<pre>'; print_r ($ _ GET); echo '</pre>';
?>
```

If you have followed the chapter on arrays well, you should know that print_r () is a function that allows you to display an array nicely. You can, therefore, conclude that $ _GET is an array. But you also notice that I did not set $ _GET. So you might think that you will have an error when testing this script: who wants to tempt the devil?

Do it all.

To reach this page, you will type in your browser a URL like http://localhost/alias/url.php or even

http://127.0.0.1/alias/url.php. When you arrive on this page, what luck, no mistake, and even text! We see this:

```
Code: Other
Array (
)
```

It won't make you the kings of the world, but it tells you something: $ _GET is an array, is defined, whereas I didn't do it in my script. Don't make those big eyes - it's completely normal! Indeed, PHP creates variables called superglobals.

This is an opportunity to make a little difference and introduce a new concept: the scope of the variables. Do you remember what I said about variables and functions?

I told you never to use variables declared out of a function in a function or vice versa. If I said that, it's because of the scope of the variables.

There are three "kinds" of variables: superglobal variables, global variables, and local variables. We will take a simple code:

```
Code: PHP
<? Php
function ()
{
$ a = $ _GET;
return $ a% 2;
}
$ b = machin ();
if (true)
{
var_dump ($ b);
}
?>
```

You will notice that I used the isset () function, which, as you should know, checks if a variable exists. If I did that, it's to avoid an error. Indeed, if I put $ _GET ['name'] directly, but instead of going to http:

//localhost/url.php? Name = something, I go to http: //localhost / url.php, what's going on? The association that has the name key is not created because it is not in my URL in the form of key = value, so I will try to use an association that does not exist: PHP me will return an undefined index error.

$ _GET is an array. Sorry to write so big, but I have to. Many people come and ask for help on the $ _GET, $ _POST, or other functions. But $ _GET and the other superglobals are not functions (there would be parentheses), they are arrays and nothing else!

Let's Keep Fit!

For this part, if you don't have HTML basics, you won't understand anything. So if you do not know what a form is, I invite you to go see another tutorial, otherwise, you will continue to struggle.

Hell of Magic Quotes

After a very interesting little blah on the XSS flaw, we will take a little time to discuss another rather annoying problem (I meant annoying, but it is not very educational!): The magic quotes.

It's a problem to talk about it here because the cause of these magic quotes (the magic_quotes) and what justified their creation is still unknown to you. So I'm going to talk about it, but very briefly. Test this code:

```php
Code: PHP
<? Php
$ text = 'lala of "and more" ". "and 'without
forgetting the'";
echo $ text;
echo addslashes ($ text);
?>
```

You see that both echoes (echo, which is a structure, not a function, I remind you) do not display the same thing. One would have guessed since one directly displays $ text, while the other displays the return value of a function: addslashes (). The purpose of this function is very simple: it adds a backslash (\) in front of these four strings: ", ', \, and NULL.

Okay, you're going to ask me what's the point of this function, I can answer you, but it would be useless because we have not yet addressed the subject. All I can say is that for a long time, this function has been the defense of many coders against a possible flaw.

But what does this have to do with the forms? Well, it's simple. In the PHP configuration file (an obscure thing that we have never seen), there are directives, that is to say, orders that the PHP must follow. One of these directives is called magic_quote_gpc. If this directive is activated, PHP will apply the addslashes () function to all the values present in the GPC arrays ($ _GET, $ _POST, and $ _COOKIE). And so, we risk ending up with an array of backslashes too!

Ideally, this directive should disappear: it was only implemented to overcome the lack of security measures of PHP coders. However, since this directive can be disabled, the configuration may change. If you are doing your script on a server that has disabled the directive, and then you decide to change the server and go to another that has activated this directive, you will have backslashes in every corner. You will have to modify your script to repair the damage.

Fortunately, version 6 of PHP will remove this directive. Unfortunately, there are lots of servers that will stay with PHP version 5 for a while, and even with PHP version 4.

I will give you a code that will allow you to have no longer to worry about magic quotes and explain it to you.

```php
Code: PHP
<? Php
if (get_magic_quotes_gpc ())
{
$ _POST = array_map ('stripslashes', $ _POST);
$ _GET = array_map ('stripslashes', $ _GET);
$ _COOKIE = array_map ('stripslashes', $ _COOKIE);
}
?>
```

The operation is very simple: first, we check if the magic_quotes are activated with the get_magic_quotes_gpc () function. If this is the case, we will use the reverse function of addlashes (): stripslashes ().

To apply a function to the set of values of an array, we use the function array_map (). The first argument is the name of the function we want to apply (stripslashes () in our case). The second argument is the array we are going to work on. This function is rudimentary and can be improved, but for the moment, it will be more than enough.

We will come back to this in Part II of this tutorial anyway, to find out why this directive exists.

I'm lost!

I will now speak very briefly about something that has nothing to do with forms or the transmission of variables: constants. If I speak about it here, it is because I had no place elsewhere. We have already heard of constants, but until now, we spoke only of constant value (for example, the constant value 5, or the constant value 'lala'). But this time, I'm going to tell you about the real constants, that is to say, the kinds of variables, whose name and value are defined once, and whose value will be impossible to modify throughout the script.

Here is how we declare a constant:

```php
Code: PHP
<? Php
define ('NOM_CONSTANTE', 'VALEUR_CONSTANTE');
echo NOM_CONSTANTE;
?>
```

To declare a constant, we use the define () function. The first argument is the name that the constant will have. The second is the value it will take (any expression).

You see that I made a weird, new instruction: echo NOM_CONSTANTE.

At first glance, you must have told me that I wanted to write a string but that I forgot to delimit it with single quotes or quotation marks. It is not so. By typing this instruction, I wanted to display the value of the constant.

To use the value of a constant, just type its name without enclosing it in quotation marks or single quotation marks. A constant is an expression like any other, just like a variable, a function that returns a value, etc. You can, therefore, use it for many things (concatenation, assignment, calculation).

When you have a variable, you can redefine its value, example:

```php
Code: PHP
<? Php
$ a = 5;
echo $ a;
$ a = 7;
echo $ a;
```

```
?>
```

This code works perfectly, but if we try to do that with constants ...

```
Code: PHP
<? php define ('A', 5);
echo A; define ('A', 7); echo A;
?>
```

Pan! A beautiful mistake is pointing the tip of his nose. It is there to tell us that we are trying to redefine the value of a constant (well, it says rather that the constant already exists).

But what interest?

I would say that there are two major cases where the constants are interesting.

The first is you want to make sure that value never changes. A value that would remain constant from the start to the end of the script. For example, to configure a script (number of news displayed per page, if you want to display signatures on a forum or not, etc.), it is very useful, because there is no risk of changing this value.

The second case is what I call dumb arguments. When you create a function, you often give it arguments, but there are times when you need to give arguments that I call mute.

Here is the list of dumb arguments:

an integer;

a floating-point number a boolean.

Why are they dumb?

Simply because we do not know what their role is, what they are used for. An example is better than a speech, and it's a gift:

```php
Code: PHP
<? Php
echo function_display_news (NB_NEWS_PAGE);
?>
Code: PHP
<? Php
echonews_display_function (20);
?>
The constant NB_NEWS_PAGE is defined as such: define
('NB_NEWS_PAGE', 20) ;.
```

Imagine that this is not your script: you come across the call of this function. Who can tell me what is the number 20 for? To display a particular category of news? To limit the number of news per page?

We cannot guess it without going to see the declaration of the function, and we waste time.

While with a constant, we have a word, a name that allows us to identify the usefulness of this parameter. When the scripts are small, and we developed them alone, the interest is limited, I admit. But when we have big scripts that we create too many, it quickly becomes the brothel, and constants can improve a little legibility of the code!

What to remember. If you only have to remember one and only one, it's the Never Trust User Input. As long as the user can not assign your script, there is almost no chance that your script poses any security problem, but as soon as the user can interact with your script, if you're not careful, it's the gateway to all sorts of security breaches.

Remember that you should never, never, never trust the user. Even if you do a member script (we will do one) and there are administrators (people you trust, in theory), you shouldn't trust them. When you make a script, anyone other than you are a potential danger. I emphasize that a lot. Security is not a story of function, but a story of behavior. You must anticipate all the possible drifts of your script and prevent them.

But do not panic, huh (): even if I want to, I will not let you wade in this case all alone, we will see the main lines of the main security holes very soon, and we will try to protect ourselves!

Chapter Five

First Lab: A Calculator

As the fourth chapter points out, it's time to take stock. We've already seen a lot of the basics of PHP together: with everything we've seen, you can do great things. In the second part of this tutorial, we will put everything into practice. But before, we will do practical work so that you can judge for yourself the state of your knowledge.

This lab is also the last chapter of Part I, so be careful.

Objectives

The purpose of this TP is that you realize a calculator. But don't worry, you're going to make it a very simple one. First, because you don't all have enough math skills to do something more complicated.

Secondly, and mainly because you are already going to drool to do something simple, I'm sure very few of you will succeed in doing something that works perfectly.

But don't worry, this lab is difficult, it's voluntary. I want you to understand for yourselves that you are not far away. You have seen the basics, but you have not practiced much yet. You therefore cruelly lack experience, and as the saying goes: "It is by forging that one becomes a blacksmith. "

So do not be surprised if you wade through semolina throughout this lab.

This calculator will be very simple. It will consist of a form with two small text boxes and a drop-down list. The textboxes will be used by the visitor to enter the two numbers he wants to process. The user will be asked to enter only whole numbers. We could take floating-point numbers, but I don't want to (and that doesn't change anything anyway!).

The drop-down list will give access to five operations, the basic operations:

addition; subtraction; division; multiplication; modulo.

Once the visitor has entered the numbers and the type of operation, your script should display the calculation and the answer.

Pay attention to the case where the visitor would like to divide (or do the modulo) by zero. Indeed, in mathematics, you cannot divide a number by zero; it gives an indefinite result. It's the same in PHP (and an error will be displayed).

You will, therefore, need to check the numbers that the visitor will enter. If he wants to divide or make the modulo by zero, you will have to display a message: an error has occurred: you cannot divide by zero. However, there is a second thing you need to check. Some browsers, via extensions, allow you to modify forms (all HTML source code, even!). We can, therefore, modify the value and company attributes. Therein lies the risk. To identify which operation to do, you will put special values in the value attributes. You will, therefore, have to check that you receive one of these values, otherwise, you will have to display the message: an error has occurred: operation undefined.

If you display one of these two errors, you should not display the calculation and the answer.

But in any case, you will always display the form so that other calculations can be made.

A Few Tips

First of all, I'm going to impose something on you: your code will have to be presented in a certain way. I will give you the skeleton of your code:

```php
Code: PHP
<? Php
/ * Declaration of constants * /
/ * Declaration of duties * /
/* Data processing */
/ * Calculation and form display * /
```

You will insert your code in these comments. If I do that, it's not to bother you, I have my reasons, but you will not know them right away. Certain sections of code may be empty, for example, the declaration of constants. I tell you plainly: there is no need for constants in this script. But keep the comment to show that you know how to separate your code and group it by "theme."

Since this is your first TP, I will be nice and give you a preview of what your code will be:

```php
Code: PHP
<? Php
/ * Declaration of constants * /
/ * Declaration of duties * /
// Create a function that will take three
parameters: the two numbers we are working on and
information that will help to know which operation
to apply
```

```php
// The function will return either a character
string or the result of the calculation
// The strings that the function can return are the
two errors I mentioned earlier
// You will have to manage the two possible errors
here
/* Data processing */
// First, you will check if all data exist and are
not empty
// To check if the variables exist, you will use one
of the two functions that we saw in the chapter on
arrays
// To check if the variables are empty, look what
returns a: trim ($ var)! = ''
// If everything is OK, you will call the function
that was declared earlier
// Depending on what the function returns, you will
need to check if an error has occurred
// To do this, just look at what type of value the
function returns to us
// If everything went well, it returns an INT,
otherwise a STRING
// To check if an expression is integer, use the
function is_int (). To check if an expression is of
type string, we use the function is_string ()
/ * Calculation and form display * /
// If the form has been submitted, you will see:
// would be an error if an error occurred,
// would be the calculation if there was no error.
// Then you will display the form
?>
```

And now, you have everything in your hands. Based on these few comments and all that you should have learned so far, you should be able to do what I ask you.

It only remains for me to wish you good luck, and good luck, especially.

Correction!

Well, if you're here, either you've done it brilliantly, or you've been miserably planted, and you give in to temptation. If you have not managed this script, but have searched for a long time (several tens of minutes at least, if not hours!), Look at the correction, it will help you.

By cons, if you have not looked, do not look! It will not bring you anything.

```php
Code: PHP
<? Php
error_reporting (E_ALL);
/ * Declaration of constants * /
/ * Declaration of duties * /
function operation ($ a, $ b, $ operation)
{
if ($ operation == 0)
{
return $ a + $ b;
}
elseif ($ operation == 1)
{
return $ a - $ b;
}
elseif ($ operation == 2)
{
return $ a * $ b;
}
elseif ($ operation && $ operation <5)
{
if ($ b! = 0)
{
if ($ operation == 3)
{
return $ a / $ b;
}
```

```php
elseif ($ operation == 4)
{
return $ a% $ b;
}
}
else
{
return 'An error has occurred: you can not divide by
zero';
}
}
else
{
}
}
return 'An error has occurred: indefinite
operation';
/* Data processing */
if (isset ($ _ POST ['a']) && trim ($ _ POST ['a'])!
= '' &&
isset ($ _ POST ['b']) && trim ($ _ POST ['b'])! =
'' &&isset ($ _ POST ['operation']) && trim ($ _
POST ['operation'])! = ' ')
{
$ display = true;
$ result = operation ((int) $ _ POST ['a'], (int) $
_ POST ['b'], (int) $ _ POST ['operation']);
$ error = is_string ($ result);
if ($ _ POST ['operation'] == 0)
{
$ sign = '+';
}
elseif ($ _ POST ['operation'] == 1)
{
$ sign = '-';
}
elseif ($ _ POST ['operation'] == 2)
{
$ sign = '*';
```

```php
}
elseif ($ _ POST ['operation'] == 3)
{
$ sign = '/';
}
else {
$ sign = '%';
}
else
{
$ display = false;
$ result = false;
$ error = false;
}
/ * Display results and form * /
if ($ display)
{
if ($ error)
{
echo $ result;
}
else
{
echo (int) $ _ POST ['a']. $ sign. (int) $ _ POST
['b']. '='.
$ Result;
}
}
?>
<form action = "index.php" method = "post">
<P>
Operand n ° 1: <input type = "text" name = "a" />
<br />
Operand n ° 2: <input type = "text" name = "b" />
<br />
Surgery :
<select name = "operation">
<option value = "0"> Addition </ option>
<option value = "1"> Subtraction </option>
```

```
<option value = "2"> Multiplication </option>
<option value = "3"> Division </ option>
<option value = "4"> Modulo </option>
</ Select>
<br />
<input type = "submit" value = "Calculate" />
</ P>
</ Form>
```

Not bad, this code, huh?

You had to get a close code, but if you do not have the same thing, it does not matter. It's even normal. The goal of the game, for the moment, is that the script works. I did not put any comments.

There are two reasons for this.

The first is that the script is ridiculously simple and short.

The second is that all the comments are a little bit above, hidden in the tips.

Now that you've had a glimpse of "real" code, I have to confess to you something: with what you know, we can do much shorter and more effective!

Can do better!

We just saw a code that works. I insist on that, it works. But it is far from ideal. This is a code that I would call simpleton; there is no reflection, no use of what we learned to simplify the script. And the logic of the script is pretty average and naive.

That's why I'm going to show you a second code: the rendering is exactly the same, but this second script is much better!

Code: PHP

```php
<? phperror_reporting (E_ALL);
/ * Declaration of constants * /
/ * Declaration of duties * /
function operation ($ a, $ b, $ operation)
{
// We check if the operation is defined
if ($ operation> = 0 && $ operation <= 4)
{
// We create an array containing three of the five operations
// We can not put the last two because if $ b is
zero, we will have an error
$ calcul = array (
$ a + $ b,
$ a - $ b,
$ a * $ b
);
// If we want to divide or make the modulo and that
$ b is equal to zero, we return an error
if ($ b == 0 && $ operation> = 3)
{
return 'An error has occurred: you can not divide by
zero';
}
// If we want to divide or do the modulo and that $
b is different from zero
// We complete the table of different possible
calculations
if ($ b! = 0 && $ operation> = 3)
{
$ calculation [] = $ a / $ b;
$ calculation [] = $ a% $ b;
}
// Finally, we return the result that corresponds to
the requested operation!
return $ calculation [$ operation];
}
else
```

```php
{
}
}
return 'An error has occurred: indefinite
operation';
/* Data processing */
// We check that all the values of the associations
contained in
$ _POST are met
$ is_valid = true; foreach ($ _ POST as $ val)
{
if (trim ($ val) == '')
{
$ is_valid = false;
}
}
// We check that the form is submitted and well
completed if (isset ($ _ POST ['a']) &&isset ($ _
POST ['b']) &&isset ($ _ POST ['operation']) && $
is_valid)
{
$ display = true;
$ result = operation ((int) $ _ POST ['a'], (int) $
_ POST ['b'], (int) $ _ POST ['operation']);
$ error = is_string ($ result);
// We use an array again to simplify processing
// We get the sign which is associated with $ _POST
['operation']
$ sign = array ('+', '-', '*', '/', '%');
if (! $ error)
{
$ sign = $ sign [(int) $ _ POST ['operation']];
}
}
else
{
$ display = false;
$ result = false;
$ error = false;
```

```php
}
/ * Display results and form * /
if ($ display)
{
if ($ error)
{
$ Result;
}
else
{
echo (int) $ _ POST ['a']. $ sign. (int) $ _ POST
['b']. '='.
$ Result;
}
}
?>
<form action = "index.php" method = "post">
<P>
Operand n ° 1: <input type = "text" name = "a" />
<br />
Operand n ° 2: <input type = "text" name = "b" />
<br />
Surgery :
<select name = "operation">
<option value = "0"> Addition </ option>
<option value = "1"> Subtraction </option>
<option value = "2"> Multiplication </option>
<option value = "3"> Division </ option>
<option value = "4"> Modulo </option>
</ Select>
<br />
<input type = "submit" value = "Calculate" />
</ P>
</ Form>
```

You are faced with two scripts that do the same thing. One is better, the second is better. But why ? First, the length. Indeed, if we omit the comments, the second script is shorter than the first one.

But hey, if it were just a story of several lines, I tell you all right: there is no point in bothering.

You notice that there are many changes in the sections on the declaration of functions and the processing of data. Indeed, the display is something relatively static: there is no way to really improve that. At best, we can gain a few microseconds and improve clarity.

It's always the data processing that takes the most time in a PHP script, so that's what you need to focus on to try to improve it. The biggest improvement in function is the decrease in the number of conditional structures. In the first script, there are six, while in the second, there are only three, half less.

But How is this Useful?

Well, when you have a conditional structure, PHP evaluates the expression between parentheses, which takes time. Less evaluation, less time lost. This is especially true in loops. Indeed, in the loops, the conditions are re-evaluated each time, so if we can remove even one of them, we could avoid a lot of useless evaluations.

To avoid having to do a lot of conditions, you see that I used an array. Indeed, the keys of this array are from 0 to 4, just like the value attributes of my form. So I can very simply retrieve the result of the calculation using an array and the value attribute value.

But I could not put the five operations right away in my array. Indeed, if I had done so, I would have had an error:

Warning: Division by zero in C: \ wamp \ www \ OwnBB \ index.php on line 93

This error tells me that on line 93, I divided a number by zero. If you encounter this error, do echo and var_dump () of your expressions to know where the problem comes from (it is thanks to these two structures/functions that we can identify most of the bugs!).

For the declaration of functions, it's over. We will now move on to data processing, which has also undergone a small facelift. The first thing that has been changed is the condition to check if the variables exist and are not empty. First of all, you must know something that I have not revealed to you yet: when a form is submitted (with a submit button or an image button), all the associations that can be created by this form exist. Whether you have completed the form or not, everything exists as soon as the form is submitted. The only exception is the checkbox, but you already know that. We can, therefore, say that if the form has not been submitted, $ _POST is an empty array; otherwise, it is an array filled with associations. However, if we remember well our notions of typecasting, we know that when we cast an array to a Boolean, two cases are possible:

if the array is empty, the boolean is false; otherwise, the boolean is true.

Now, the foreach: you know that it is used to traverse an array. What is good with this structure is that it does not generate an error if the array passed to it is empty.

Before my foreach, I create a Boolean variable that is true.

I run the table, and I assign to this variable the return of trim ($ val) == ".

This expression can return either true or false. If the variable consists of spaces only or if it is empty, it returns true, otherwise false.

Clearly, if only one of the values in $ _POST is empty (the empty string " or a string made only of spaces),

$ is_valid will be false.

I did not have to show you that it does not have much interest here. But when you have to check if forty small text boxes are filled, it will be very useful for you.

The condition, you must understand it: we check that $ _POST is not empty and that all the fields are filled. The second big improvement is the removal of the five conditions! It is summed up in one thanks to the arrays for the second time.

This second script is cleaner and more efficient than the first. What I want you to understand is that there is always a way to see a problem from another angle. The goal of the game is to find the angle that will give you the most effective solution. This search for the most effective solution is called optimization.

In PHP, the best way to optimize your code (as fast as possible), is to review its logic, to try to remove expensive structures in performance (such as conditions, loops, functions heavy ...).

Many people will give you little "tricks," like using "instead of" to delineate your strings. This kind of "thing" is not wrong; it's true. But the time you will gain is really insignificant compared to what you could gain by reviewing your logic. That's why I do not call this kind of optimization practice, but DIY, quibble.

It's like you have to go from Paris to Marseille. You have a 2 CV, you ask your neighbor: "In your opinion, I would go faster if I inflate my tires a little? It will only save you a few minutes.

Whereas if you review your logic and take the TGV instead of this car, you would gain dozens of hours. Now, when you look at a script, you'll always have to ask yourself, "Can not we improve it? You don't have to settle for something that works; you always have to aim for performance. And besides, there is probably still a way to improve this second script. After all, maybe I did not have the angle of view that would improve all that.

If you've done it right the first time, congratulations, that's fine.

If you have had to look for a little or even a lot, but you have done it anyway, I congratulate you even more because you have done your best and persevered. For those who have totally missed the TP, do not worry. It is by coding that one becomes a coder.

To be honest, I never did a single tutorial that taught me the basics of PHP, and that didn't stop me from going far enough. If you are hot for Part II, which looks very entertaining, what are you still doing there?

Chapter Six

MySQL, PHP, And MySQL

Behind many PHP scripts, there is something almost unavoidable: a database. That's what MySQL is. You will quickly understand how this tool is convenient!

But before mixing PHP and MySQL, we will start by learning how to use MySQL.

What is MySQL?

So far, you have learned the basics of PHP, a web-oriented scripting language. Only, although you have acquired several concepts, several tools, the scripts that you can create at the moment are quite limited. We will remedy this by giving you the possibility of creating scripts that you probably already know: news scripts, guestbook scripts, online counter, etc.

A database is not essential to do all this; you can get by without it. But the strength of a database will greatly facilitate the development of these scripts.

What You Need To Know About MySQL

MySQL, I told you it is a database. Lack of luck, I already lied to you. If MySQL was just a database, I tell you all right: we would have no interest in using it.

The interest of MySQL lies in the fact that it is a Relational Database Management System, which I will henceforth abbreviate as RDBMS.

But What Is An RDBMS?

An RDBMS is a database structured according to relational principles. A database (which I will abbreviate in BDD) is a structured and organized whole that allows the storage and the exploitation of a large amount of information, data.

But What Is The Interest?

Let's take a concrete example: a forum. In a forum, you have categories, topics, and messages. The subjects belong to the categories, and the messages belong to the subjects. There are, therefore, relationships between these three elements.

If we don't use an RDBMS, we will set up a whole management system with files in PHP (we will see how to handle files with PHP later). Only this system will be very long and complex to set up, which is rather boring. What is more, to develop such a system, functional and efficient, it is not within reach of the first comer. It takes experience and a lot of knowledge to handle all the scenarios.

Now, if we use an RDBMS, what are we going to do? First, we will not create a management system. Indeed, we already have one available: the RDBMS. All you, the creators of the script, will have to do is give orders to the RDBMS ("create such a subject in such a category," "give me the list of messages for the subject," "delete this," etc.). The advantages are multiple, but in priority, I would quote the ease of use, the performances, and the possibilities of management.

The goal of the game, it will be to teach you how to communicate with an RDBMS, and more particularly with MySQL. Indeed, to communicate with MySQL, we will have to learn a new language: SQL.

Yes, you're out of luck, you're not done yet.

But why another language? The reason is simple: RDBMS is organized in a certain way, so you cannot do everything and anything in any way, there are procedures to be followed so that the RDBMS does the right thing.

This time, it will not be the case: I will not teach you how to master RDBMS, but I will show you how to use it. If I do that, it's simply because I don't know enough about RDBMS to do a tutorial that would explain everything about everything.

But do not worry, what follows will meet the expectations of 99.99% of you. For those who stay, you will just have to find a complete tutorial or go and read the documentation.

Are we getting organized?

The first concept to acquire to use an RDBMS is the structural organization of the databases. MySQL is a software, as well as Firefox, Kopete, Windows Media Player. But MySQL has only one goal: to manage databases. The number of databases MySQL can manage has only one limit: the space available on your hard drive. Suffice to say that before filling all that, you'll have tons of databases. If we had to make an analogy with the real world, imagine a building. In this building, you have several rooms: each of these rooms is a database.

But these bases are also organized! They are organized into tables. Each table has its own name, and it is linked to the database to which it belongs. These tables are themselves organized like a filing cabinet (or a table): in columns and in rows.

These four organizational notions (base, table, column, and line) form the basis of everything. It is the foundation of the organization of a database.

To use the analogy of earlier, if the rooms are the databases, then there are cabinets in these rooms. The cabinets represent the tables. Each cabinet has different drawers; these are the lines. And in these drawers, there are different compartments; these are the columns. And in each compartment, there is data. And of course, the type of compartments, their number, size, etc. are the same for all drawers in the cabinet.

Blue delimits the database. The two green rectangles are two tables. The one above is a table that would contain a list of members, for example. There are three columns to this table: "pseudo," "password," and "signature." In this table, there are two tuples, two rows of data.

The second table could contain news. There would be two columns, "title" and "content," and only one news (one line and one news per line).

The scheme is ugly, but the important thing is that you understand the general organization.

The console at any age

Before we start in the SQL, you should launch the right software.

If you are on Linux, it's very simple. You just have to open a terminal and type: MySQL -u root.

If you are on Windows, it can be very simple or a little less. But we will have a little fun! First of all, you will have to find a file, an executable: mysql.exe.

Then, you will need to find the folder in which you installed the webserver (WAMP, EasyPHP, etc.). Generally, it is at the root of the hard drive or in the Program Files folder. For example, at home, I access the WAMP file with path C: \Wamp\. Once you have this path, you will open the Windows command prompt. To do this, a shortcut: press the "Windows" key and the "R" key simultaneously. Type cmd in the command prompt and validate it!

You should see the Windows console open before your eyes. Now we will launch the MySQL console! First, type this:

```
Code: Console
cd "C: \ Wamp \ MySQL \ bin \" MySQL -u root
```

If you cannot do something similar, start again from the beginning, you must have been wrong in the path of the folder.

Now, let everyone look. In theory, you are the supreme gods who can do anything on databases.

But check this by typing this in the console:

Code: SQL

SHOW DATABASES; CREATE DATABASE test; SHOW DATABASES;

DROP DATABASE test;

SHOW DATABASES;

If you do not get something close (only the names of the databases could differ), it means that you are not logged in as root. If this is the case, reread the game on the opening of the console!

If you only had to remember two things in this chapter, it would be this:

PHP and SQL are two distinct languages that are completely independent of each other. A database is organized into tables, which is organized in rows and columns.

After this short introduction, we will accelerate the pace and set off to discover SQL!

Before we can work on a database, we need a database! But as it is very simple and fast, we will also learn to create a table. In the example, it will be a table to manage messages from a guest book (a TP that we will do soon!). Be very attentive and reread, reread, reread again and again because the creation of the tables is not particularly complex, but there are several things to remember.

The base above all

As I told you in the previous chapter, MySQL is a database manager, so we will naturally start by creating one. To do this, open your MySQL console, as I explained in the previous chapter.

If you are there, enter these queries in the console:

Code: SQL

SHOW DATABASES; CREATE DATABASE test; SHOW DATABASES;

SHOW DATABASES; is a query that returns the list of databases that MySQL handles. As you can see in the picture, my first SHOW DATABASES; I return seven bases (information_schema, dev, MySQL, ngu, ownbb, phpmyadmin, and softbb).

MySQL also sends me a message, seven rows in a set game (or more exactly, result set) is the set of rows that a query returns.

I told you that a database is organized in rows and columns, well it's the same for queries. Queries that return a result always return a result set that is organized in rows and columns. If you look at the picture, you can notice that the list of my bases is presented in table form. Each database has its own row. And at the very top of the list is the header of the table where you can read "Database."

Remember the previous chapter, when I told you that each column had a name, well, it's the same for queries. The result set of a query is organized in rows and columns, and each column has a name. And you'll see later why it's so important that queries give the columns a name.

Then I create a base called test with the CREATE DATABASE test;

MySQL then sends me a message, Query OKOK, 1 Row Affected. MySQL tells me that my request has been executed and that this query has assigned a line. The previous query returned a result set, but not this one. In fact, there are two main types of queries: those that return a result and those that affect and modify existing data. By modification, it is also the creation, the deletion, the modification of data, etc.

When you use one of these queries that affect rows, MySQL returns the number of rows your query has assigned. Here, we create a base, so we assign one and only one line. It is often interesting to know how many lines a request affect. It can be used in particular to resolve errors in your code. But it allows many other things. The third query is no longer unknown. It returns a result set that contains the list of bases. And as expected, we have a base that has been added to the others, the test base. So we have two proofs that this database was created. Now, we are going to provoke an error that will allow me to tackle two theoretical points, one of which is very close to my heart: prefixing.

The error is quite simple to understand. The test database already exists, we are trying to create a database with the same name, MySQL returns an error that says that the database already exists, it is completely logical.

The first thing I want to talk to you about is an option. If you try to create a database that already exists, you will be entitled to an error. Only you will sometimes have to create a database without knowing if it already exists. So you have two possibilities: the first, we play it safe, we check that the database does not exist before creating it. The second, more expeditious, is to create the table and see if we have an error. Only these two possibilities are boring and ugly: the first forces us to make two requests, and the second could generate errors. That's why MySQL provides us with a third possibility: to create the database if it does not already exist.

Hop, magic, no more mistakes!

But a problem arises then: how to know if the base already existed?

As you can see, MySQL tells us that no line has been assigned. And that's how you can tell if the database already existed: by looking at the number of rows that the query has affected.

We will now talk about prefixing, which is a convention that I set for myself. You are absolutely not required to follow it, but it is a practice that I find extremely useful. A prefix is a particle placed at the beginning of a word to modify its meaning. Imagine that you use two applications in PHP that need to create a base, and imagine that by chance, both applications give the same name to their base. You will have a problem since you cannot create two databases with the same name. And this is where the prefixing comes in: by adding a particle in front of the name of the base, the problem disappears!

If the two applications wanted to call their base lala, we would have had a problem. But now, as each of the applications gives a prefix, for example, ooo_ and uuu_, the problem no longer arises since the bases are called ooo_lala and uuu_lala.

Well, in reality, applications in PHP rarely create bases, so the prefixing of database names is of little interest. But when we play with tables, columns, joins, etc., you will see how prefixing the names of bases, tables, and columns can make many requests easier. Before moving on to creating tables, I will still show you a query and tell you a word about the name of the databases. If it is useful to know how to create a base, it is also useful to be able to delete one. It just tells us that we cannot delete the 'test' database because it does not exist.

Be very careful with the drop. It's very practical, but it's completely irreversible. If you delete a database, you delete everything in it, including tables and data. So be sure of what you are doing! (We will learn to make a backup in a short time.)

In PHP, there was a convention for naming its variables. Well, it's the same for the name of the tables. To understand this convention, you have to know one thing: when you create a database, you actually create a folder on your hard disk (which has the name of your database) in the \ MySQL \ data directory \ (my home is in c: \ Wamp \ MySQL \ data \). The naming convention is simple. You can use any character allowed in a folder name, except the slash (/), backslash (\), and period (.).

However, it is still a convention that I set for myself, but do not give too odd names to your tables. Ideally, limit yourself to alphabetic characters and underscore (_).

Let's sit down?

Now that we have the basics, we're going to create a table. Nothing could be simpler, I can assure you. The little request of my heart:

The main course!

We will tackle the biggest chunk of this chapter: the creation of the table structure. It is both the simplest and the most complicated of the topics in this chapter. It's simple because if you manage to represent the structure of a table, you will have no difficulty. It's complicated because there are a lot of keywords to remember, as well as various little things.

The simplest way to guide you in the meanders of the structure of a table, it is to start from a request which creates a table to touch a little with all. But before giving you this request, we will take the time to think about what we want to do. We want to make a table to collect messages from a guestbook.

The first question to ask is: "What are we going to have to put in this table?" "

The first thing is obvious: the message itself. The message is a text, a character string of variable length (it can be very short as very long).

Second very useful thing, the nickname of the author of the message. This nickname is also a string, but we can consider that it is a string containing few characters (I have rarely seen nicks of more than 50 or 100 characters).

The third piece of information that interests us: the date. This is new to you. We never saw how to use dates, neither in PHP nor in SQL. In SQL, dates are a particular type of data; they are data of type ... date. Yes, in SQL, too, we find this typing story. We will add two more columns to this table. The first is indispensable, the second optional (but still very useful).

The optional column will be used to record the IP (we saw what it was at the very beginning) of the postmaster of the message when he posted it. The main interest is to be able to find who posted the message (although it is difficult, if not almost impossible) in case we need it (for example, if he posted a bad message). We have seen that the IP is in the form of four numbers separated by dots. So it's a string of characters. However, you should know that we can convert the IP to an integer, and we will do it. The column will, therefore, store whole numbers. You will see why it is more interesting to store the IP as an integer later.

These four columns were quite obvious; there is nothing unnatural. But the fifth is a little strange at first sight. When you have a lot of messages in your guestbook, you may receive harmful messages (insults, spam, etc.) that you must delete. Only, how are we going to tell MySQL which message to delete?

It would require information that would be unique, that would be specific to each message.

We could use other things to identify the message, the nickname, for example, or the IP. Unfortunately, we cannot be sure that there will not be two messages with the same IP or the same nickname, and if that happens, we could accidentally delete a message that should not be.

So we will use a number: each message will match a number, it will be its identifier (abbreviated id). This number will be incremented by 1 with each new message posted: thus, we will never have two messages having the same number. And to delete a message, we just need to know the number that corresponds to it!

As you have probably understood, this fifth column will, therefore, store numbers.

Now that you know what we are going to put in this table, here is without delay the coveted request:

```sql
Code: SQL
CREATE TABLE dev_gbook (
gbook_id INT UNSIGNED NULL AUTO_INCREMENT PRIMARY
KEY,
gbook_ip INT NOT NULL,
gbook_msg TEXT NOT NULL, gbook_pseudo VARCHAR (100)
NOT NULL, gbook_date DATETIME NOT NULL
);
```

If you see a table with dev_gbook as the only line, OKOK: everything is good!

As you can see, as for the names of databases and tables, I added a prefix (the name of the table without its prefix) in front of the names of all my columns. The main interest is to avoid ambiguous names. Later, we will manipulate several tables at the same time: two, three, four, or more. Imagine that you have two tables with a column for an identifier (id). If you name both id columns, how will MySQL know which column you are talking about?

With the name of the prefix table, you will never have this problem.

The second advantage is that it will save you from mistakes. Imagine if I did not put the prefix. The name of my columns would have been: id, ip, msg, pseudo, and date. But lack of luck, for MySQL, DATE has a particular meaning (as in PHP, I cannot give any name to my functions), and it will return you a nice syntax error (yes, SQL queries follow a very precise syntax).

After this little interlude, we will go to the most important point: the request that creates our table. I'll explain all this gibberish.

This request tells MySQL to create a table named dev_gbook. The table structure will be put in parentheses. Next, come five lines. As you can imagine, each line tells MySQL to add a column.

Lack of luck, the first is the most complex of all. I will come back to this later! We will rather start with the third:

First, you see the name of the column, gbook_msg. Just after the column name, we indicate the type of the column. Here, we want a type that would allow us to store a text of variable length (which can be very long): the most common column type suitable is, therefore, the TEXT type.

Then come two keywords, NOT and NULL. Putting a NOT NULL means that you will not be able to put a NULL value in the table (this is an approximation, I will come back to this later). If you simply put NULL, you can put NULL in your table (there are cases in which to use NULL is useful, for example, if I wanted to give the possibility to give or not a note, 8/10 for example, in the guestbook).

Do not put NOT NULL or NULL will not cause an error, but it's like putting NULL.

If you understand the explanation above, you should be able to understand this line. First, we indicate the name of the column, gbook_date, its type, DATETIME, and finally, we say that we cannot put a NULL.

In this column, well-known things like the name, gbook_pseudo, and the NOT NULL. The only thing that differs is the guy. The VARCHAR type is a type of column that allows you to store from 0 to 255 characters, so it is to store a fairly short string. But what is the

100 in parentheses? This is simply the maximum number of characters that can be stored in this column. If you try to store a string of 101 characters, the string will be cut off, and only the first 100 characters will be saved. If you know the maximum number of characters (for example, if you impose nicknames of 20 characters maximum), it is in your best interest to put this number in parentheses. When MySQL reads your data, if it knows that there is a maximum of 20 characters, it will only have to read 20 characters. But if you did not indicate an adequate size, that you put 255 for example, MySQL will read 255 characters to recover 20 of them (again, it is an approximation, but the idea is there).

Very simple: we create a column called gbook_ip of integer type (INT) and which cannot contain a NULL. Now that you're a little more familiar with the column descriptions, we'll be able to go back to the first one:

I'm going to break down the line:

gbook_id;

INT UNSIGNED; NOT NULL; AUTO_INCREMENT; PRIMARY KEY.

The first thing you know is the name.

The second is, as always, the type. But if you recognize the keyword INT, which indicates an integer column,

you don't know what UNSIGNED is, and what it is for.

Have you ever wondered how your computer differentiates a positive integer from a negative integer? Well, it's very simple. When your computer stores a negative whole number, it stores the positive whole number and a small piece of information (a signature, the sign) in addition, which indicates that it is a negative number.

Concretely, if you need five bits to store a positive number, you will need six bits to store the corresponding negative number, so the signature is one bit, called a sign bit. The number of bits MySQL uses to store an INT, and an UNSIGNED INT is the same, but with an UNSIGNED INT, you tell MySQL that the number is always positive, so the sign bit is useless, which saves you a bit for storing the number, which allows you to store larger numbers. You will see this in the next chapter.

NOT NULL, no need to add more.

Now a new keyword: AUTO_INCREMENT. If you look at this word, you see INCREMENT; it is quite close to something that we know: incrementation. Remember, I told you that to identify each message, we would use a number that is incrementing. Only, it would be heavy: it would make a request to recover the largest number. This is why MySQL added an option that allows you not to have to worry about that: auto-incrementing. When you store a message, thanks to auto-incrementation, we won't have to worry about the id to assign to the message, MySQL will take care of it for us.

Auto-incrementing works, of course, only with integer columns.

The last two keywords, PRIMARY and KEY, are also unknown to you. For now, we will forget about them. Just know that when you put the AUTO_INCREMENT option on a column, you must add the PRIMARY KEY option (this is not entirely true, but for now, consider that it is like this).

And there you are: you now know how to create a table and columns. There are several other types of columns; you should always use the type that is best for storing your data. If you need to store a number, use an INT column and not VARCHAR. Both work, but the INT type column is much lighter and faster.

Well, you seem to have learned a bunch of things. If you have any doubts, do not hesitate to read and re-read again and again, as the next chapter will be based almost exclusively on the types of columns and options. A small gift that will allow you to test by creating tables with different columns:

It should help you to visualize the different columns of a table, their type, if they can be null, etc.

Despite and because of the amount of information in this chapter, there is no MCQ. The key points of this chapter are:

the concept of result sets;

creation and deletion of databases; the obligation to tell MySQL what we are working on; the notion of the type of columns;

the notion of column option (NULL / NOT NULL, AUTO_INCREMENT); the naming conventions for databases, tables, and columns.

Manage our tables!

In the previous chapter, we saw how to create a simple table. But I have not shown you all types of columns, and I have not said anything about the management of the table after it was created.

By management, I mean a little bit of everything: add a column, delete, modify, etc.!

A very interesting chapter that will allow you to start to really manipulate the tables.

A whole story.

It is time to leave the practice a bit to go back to the good old theory. As I told you, always use the type of column that best fits the type of data you will be storing. That's why MySQL provides us with a very large number of column types, nearly thirty.

First, I'll give you a query that does not work, but that represents all types of columns and their options:

```sql
Code: SQL
CREATE TABLE table_name (
column_namecolumn_type [NULL | NOT NULL] [DEFAULT
default_value] [AUTO_INCREMENT] [[PRIMARY] KEY]
[COMMENT 'comment']
);
```

First, table_name is logically the name of the table you are going to create. Then comes col_name: this is the name you give to a column. Then, we have type_colonne, which indicates the type of the column. which we will see all the possible types later.

Now we start serious things: first, hooks. When something is put in square brackets, it is optional and you don' have to put it in. And you see, the hooks can nest.

Second thing, the vertical bar (|), aka the pipe. When you have several possible values for the same element, they are separated by a vertical bar.

After the type of the column, you can find either a NULL or a NOT NULL. I already explained to you how these keywords were, so I do not come back on it.

But here's a little new: DEFAULT. Imagine that you make a news system with news validation (that is, an administrator must allow the news to be displayed so that it is visible to everyone). To differentiate a piece of validated news from a piece of non-validated news, you would use an additional column which could take two states, validated or not (we will see later what type of column corresponded to this data). Only, you must realize that most of the time, when we add news, it will not be validated. The column that contains this information will, therefore, very often have the same information when we insert the news in the table. And I do not know about you, but I find it boring always to have to tell MySQL that the news is not validated.

That's why MySQL allows us to use default values. If we do not inform the value of a column that has a default value, MySQL will store the default value; otherwise, it will store the value we give it. It must remind you of something, right? Yes! The functions in PHP: remember, we could give a default value to one or more parameters; it's the same with MySQL.

To use the example of the guestbook table, we could have set a default value on a column: the one that stores the date.

But it's a variable date, right?

Yes, the date on which the message is posted varies, but how the date is obtained does not vary (in reality, we use a function of MySQL: yes, yes, in SQL, also there are functions). When you can use a default, do so. Your queries will be shorter and faster to execute.

Default_value is, of course, to be replaced by the default value.

The next option, also optional and known, is auto-incrementation. I do not come back either, but I remind you anyway that we can use auto-incrementation only on columns type integer! Here's something we've seen before, but I have not talked about it in detail, and I will not do it now. For the time being, just remember that you do not have to use this option except on columns that have auto-increment.

Last keyword: HOW. The latter is used to comment on a column, on its role. Sometimes the names of the columns are not very explicit (if I name my column gbook_ivba, you do not know what it's used for!), And it's quite difficult to know what is the purpose of one or the other. But if you put a comment, it will be a breeze (but hey, the best is to give explicit names).

So much for the bulk of the query, we will now move on to something equally interesting: the types of columns!

Let's start smoothly with columns of integer types. Yes, there are several types of columns to store whole numbers, five exactly: TINYINT, SMALLINT, MEDIUMINT, INT, and BIGINT.

If I tell you that storing the number 200 takes a lot less space than storing the 2,000,000,000 number, do you agree?

MySQL is. If you don't tell it that you're storing a small number, MySQL will need to read more information to make sure it reads the whole number, that it doesn't forget a chunk of it. And so, if the number is small, MySQL will read data for nothing, which is a waste of time. That's why MySQL allows us to specify the size of the number with these five types. More precisely, these types make it possible to store a number included in an interval (roughly, the number which one wants to store must be comprised between a smaller number and a larger number, which are called the bounds). Here are the intervals:

Column	type	Interval
TINYINT	from	- 128 to + 127
SMALLINT	from	- 32 768 to + 32 767

```
MEDIUMINT    from                - 8 388 808 to + 8 388
807
INT                 from              - 2,147,483,648 to
+ 2,147,483,647
BIGINT                       - 9 223 372 036 854 775 808
to + 9 223 372 036 854 775 807
```

As you can see, the intervals are rather varied, and some are really huge. When you store a number, you will always have to ask yourself, "What is the maximum value I could store? ".

There are cases where it is very simple, for example, in the case of a column used to store a percentage of success. Since the limit is 100%, the maximum value is 100. The most suitable column type is TINYINT.

Unfortunately, it is not always easy to find this maximum value, for example, for the message-id of your guestbook. How many will there be? 100? 1,000? 10,000?

In this kind of case, do not hesitate to use the INT type (when you have more than two billion messages, you will call me), which is more than enough in most cases.

So you know five types of columns, well I must admit something: you actually know ten, the double!

Why? Because of the UNSIGNED. I told you about the difference between the type INT and INT UNSIGNED in the previous chapter: it's the same for these five types, we can put them in UNSIGNED.

And in reality, the only thing that changes between an integer and an integer UNSIGNED is the bounds of the interval. The lower bound is 0 (the lowest positive integer), and the upper bound is 0

Column	type	Interval
TINYINT	UNSIGNED	from 0 to 255
SMALLINT	UNSIGNED	from 0 to 65,535
MEDIUMINT	UNSIGNED	from 0 to 16,777,615
INT	UNSIGNED	from 0 to 4,294,967,295
BIGINT	UNSIGNED	from 0 to 18 446 744 073 709 551 615

If you've been paying attention to the upper bounds, you may have noticed three things.

First, the upper bounds are equal to twice the upper bound of the corresponding columns without the UNSIGNED plus 1. For example, for TINYINT, the upper bound was 127. With the formula, we have as upper bound for the TINYINT UNSIGNED: (2 * 127) +1 = 254 + 1.

The second is that the upper bound is also equal to a certain power of 2 minus 1 (for those who do not yet know what the powers are, 2 power 3 is equal to 2 * 2 * 2, 2 power 7 equals 2 * 2 * 2 * 2 * 2 * 2 * 2). For TINYINT UNSIGNED, the upper bound is 255 = 256-1 = (2 ^ 16) -1.

The third thing is that the upper bound is equal to the sum of the absolute values of the two bounds of the corresponding column type without the UNSIGNED. For those who do not yet know what the absolute value is, the absolute value of -3 is equal to 3, the absolute value of -4 is equal to 4, the absolute value of 5 is equal to 5. For the TINYINT UNSIGNED, the upper bound is equal to 255 = | -128 | + | 127 | = 128 + 127.

It's already not bad.

But if we advance well, we have not quite finished with these integers. In addition to having five types of columns, one can also specify the number of digits that the number one wants to store may contain. Re-read this sentence once or twice. Just in case, I do a little deviation to recall the difference between a number and a number. A number is a symbol that represents a numeric value. In the decimal system, there are only ten digits: 0, 1, 2, 3, 4, 5, 6, 7, 8, 9.

A number is a concept that represents a unit, a collection of units, or a fraction of a unit. 65 is a number, for example. A number is written with numbers, but a number is not written with numbers. So let's go back to our columns. I told you that you could tell MySQL the number of digits that make up a number. You will understand the interest in a few lines: here is how to indicate the number of digits that make up a number.

If you try to store the number 9999, this number will be stored. But then, what interest?

The interest is zero-fill. Imagine that you want to insert numbers with zeros in front, 004, for example. If you use what I have taught you so far, you will never be able to retrieve anything other than 4, although you are trying to store 004.

To do this, MySQL has provided another option, zero-fill. If you are using ZEROFILL, MySQL will add 0 before the number until you get the number of digits that can make up the numbers stored in the column. For example, I want to store the number 0004.

As you can see, I put the UNSIGNED and the ZEROFILL in square brackets, they are optional, and I will not explain their role since it is already seen.

The only novelty is DECIMAL.

For integers, we could tell MySQL how many digits we wanted to store in a column; we can do the same with decimals. But on top of that, you can also tell MySQL how many digits after the decimal point you want to keep.

In my example, I create a column of type DECIMAL that can contain five-digit numbers, with two decimal places.

So, if I try to store 999999.99999, MySQL will store 999.99. If I try to store 55.5555555, MySQL will store 55.56 (when MySQL truncates a number, it rounds it off).

Now, let's move on with columns that will allow us to store dates, times, and so on.

We have already seen a type of column for storing a date, the DATETIME type. It can store dates in this format: YYYY-MM-DD HH: MM: SS. It is an English format (there we indicate the year, then the month, then the day, then the hours, then the minutes, then the seconds). Don't worry, we'll see how to change this format.

There are other types of columns for dates. Suppose you only need the year, the month and the day. It would be quite useless to store the time since it is not desired. We will, therefore, use another type, DATE. This type of column allows you to store a date in YYYY-DD-MM format.

There are still other types of columns, the TIMESTAMP type, for example. It is a type quite close to the DATETIME type, but some differences remain.

Just like with numbers, the dates you can store are limited by two bounds. For a column of type DATETIME, you can store dates between 1000-01-01 00:00:00 and 9999-12-31 23:59:59, so from midnight on January 1 of the year 1000 to 23 hours 59 minutes 59 seconds on December 31, 9999, there is room.

For the DATE type, you can store dates between 1000-01-01 and 9999-12-31, and for the TIMESTAMP type, it goes from January 1, 1970, until approximately the year 2037.

Now let's move on to the fourth type of time column, the TIME type. This type can cause problems of understanding if we are not careful, we will see why.

We saw the DATE type and the DATETIME type, we saw that the DATE type is a part of the DATETIME type, so we can assume that TIME is the missing part.

And it's not wrong, but it's incomplete. In addition to storing time in the format HH: MM: SS, the TIME type is ideal for storing a time, for example, 106 hours 23 minutes 43 seconds.

Imagine that you make a table for durations of the crossing of France on horseback (this is an example), you may have 36 hours 20 minutes, but you can also have 300 hours 56 minutes 06 seconds. The best type of column to store this information is TIME.

But that's not all! You can also store a negative duration. I do not have an example of use at hand, but it does not matter.

You can store durations/hours between -838: 59: 59 and 838: 59: 59, so from -838 hours 59 minutes 59 seconds to 838 hours 59 minutes 59 seconds.

Let's finish with the dates with the fifth and last type of time column, type YEAR. This type of column is used to store dates in YYYY format between 1901 and 2155 (but do not ask me why).

Without further ado, let's talk about the columns used to store strings. We have already seen one of these types: the VARCHAR. This column is used to store strings with a maximum of 255 characters, but we have seen that this limit could be reduced. For example, if instead of 255 characters:

There is another type very close to VARCHAR, the CHAR type. For you, the two types are strictly identical (it is also necessary to specify the maximum number of characters that can be stored there, the maximum limit is 255), the only difference lies in the way MySQL stores them. I advise you to use the VARCHAR as it is generally more economical in terms of place on the hard disk (the only case where it is heavier is when you store strings that have the maximum number of characters allowed: therefore, if you are certain that the majority of the data in the column will have the maximum number of characters allowed, using a CHAR is more economical).

After the short texts, we will move on to the longer texts with the TEXT type and its three brothers. Why three brothers? It is quite simply that the TEXT type, just like the INT type, has several identical types, the only difference being the maximum number of characters that can be stored there. These three brothers are TINYTEXT, MEDIUM TEXT, and LONGTEXT.

And here is a table with the character limit:

Column type Maximum number of characters

```
TINYTEXT 256
TEXT 65,536
MEDIUMTEXT 16,777,216
LONGTEXT 4 294 967 296
```

You may have noticed, once again, the limits are powers of 2 ($2 \wedge 8$, $2 \wedge 16$, $2 \wedge 24$, and $2 \wedge 32$). In fact, there is a huge amount of mathematics hidden behind databases, but that is not the subject.

The following type is a bit special as it is used to store everything you want in binary form. You could, for example, use it to store an image, but in practice, we will not do it. I will probably show you no example in which this type of column will be needed. This particular type is BLOB. And just like the TEXT type, he has three brothers: TINYBLOB, MEDIUMBLOB, and LONGBLOB.

Courage: there are only two types!

The type we are interested in now will allow you to insert data that belongs to a list. Let's take the example of news validated or not. The only two possible data are validated and not validated. With this type, if we try to insert another data than one of these two, MySQL will store an empty string. This particular type is ENUM.

To create a column of this type, here's how to do it:

You can put 65,535 (= (2 ^ 16) -1, when I told you that mathematics is everywhere) possible elements in an ENUM. And the -1 in (2 ^ 16) -1 is explained simply by the fact that if you try to store an unauthorized value, MySQL will store an empty string (basically, if you specify three possible values, it comes back to specify four because MySQL can store an empty string). As a consequence of that, it is, of course, totally useless to allow to store an empty string, since MySQL already does it when it is necessary.

The last type, SET, is a little more complex than the others, so I will not talk about it. And anyway, it is quite rare to use it.

A little gift, a list of all types of columns with their options!

```
TINYINT [(number of digits)] [UNSIGNED] [ZEROFILL]
SMALLINT [(number of digits)] [UNSIGNED] [ZEROFILL]
MEDIUMINT [(number of digits)] [UNSIGNED] [ZEROFILL]
INT [(number of digits)] [UNSIGNED] [ZEROFILL]
INTEGER [(number_of_digits)] [UNSIGNED] [ZEROFILL]
BIGINT [(number_of_digits)] [UNSIGNED] [ZEROFILL]
```

```
DECIMAL (number_of_digits, number_of_digits_after
the comma) [UNSIGNED] [ZEROFILL] DATE
TIME TIMESTAMP DATETIME
CHAR (number of characters) VARCHAR (number of
characters) TINYBLOB
BLOB MEDIUMBLOB LONGBLOB TINY TEXT TEXT MEDIUMTEXT
LONGTEXT
ENUM ('value_1', 'value_2', 'value_3', ...)
```

With all that, whoever dares to choose a wrong type of column, I bite it.

There are a few other types that are aliases (different names for the same type of columns), and one or two options that I didn't mention, but it will come later.

And management?

It's nice all that, but now we will practice all this theory to manage our tables a little. For the moment, you know how to create a table, but once created, it's over, you're cooked.

The first thing we will do is learn how to delete a table.

Be very careful: just like when you delete a database, if you delete a table, you also delete all the data that the table contains.

So let's test this. We will first create a table, then delete it. And we will display the list of tables each time to see what happens.

```
Code: SQL
USE dev_dev;
SHOW TABLES;
CREATE TABLE test (TEXT test);
SHOW TABLES; DROP TABLE test; SHOW TABLES;
```

By carefully looking at what the SHOW TABLES; returns to us, we can see that the table is created and then deleted.After deleting a table, we will see how to modify a table. I'm going to teach you how to do four things: delete a column, add a column, change a column, and finally change the type of a column.

Okay, no more blah, we're going to start playing. We will work on the table dev_gbook that I made you create in the previous chapter. In reality, I voluntarily slipped a small error into it. I told you that we would transform the entire IP using a PHP function, only, this function can return a negative number. However, the column which will store the IP, gbook_ip, is of type INT UNSIGNED. We cannot, therefore, store a negative number there. We will play with this column to illustrate the management of a table.

We will start with something fairly simple; we will delete this column. Here is a generic request to delete any column:

Code: SQL

ALTER TABLE table_name DROP COLUMN col_name;

I told you that in PHP, it was necessary to put only one instruction per line. In SQL, sometimes, we get queries that are simply monstrous with tons of tricks. In this kind of case, typing everything on one line is quite crippling, and it makes the query difficult to read.

This is why I got into the habit of putting line breaks and indentations even in my requests.

I don't know about you, but I much prefer my last request to the previous one, it is much airier and pleasant to read. And of course, these three lines form one and only one query, since there is only a semicolon (which serves, I remind you, to mark the end of a query).

Over time, you will begin to feel when to add line breaks or indentations without even looking at your request. In short, we were at the creation of a column. The ALTER TABLE nom_table is not unknown to you; it indicates that we are modifying (alter) a table (table).

The ADD COLUMN keywords indicate that you want to add a column. col_name is the name of the future column, type_col is its type, and option_col is options (NULL, NOT NULL, and so on). The novelty is what's in the square brackets in the third line. Imagine that you are responsible for organizing the implementation of products in a radius of a supermarket: how will you know where to place salads in relation to fruits, fruits, compared to chocolates, etc.??

We will have to tell you, give you an order to respect. For the columns of a table, it's the same. We create them in a particular order (the order in which we define them when we create the table), and this order does not change. If we want to add a column, we must tell MySQL where to put this column.

That's what the hooks are for. But as you can see, it's in brackets, so that means it's optional. In fact, let us take the example of the rays, we could say to the person who ranks: if you do not know where it's going, put it at the end of the ray.

Well, it's the same with MySQL: if you do not tell him where to put this new column, he will put it after the others, at the end, in the last position.

Now, let's look at the two possibilities that are hidden in its brackets: we have two keywords. The first is FIRST: if you put this keyword, MySQL will put this column in the first position, which is quite logical.

Now we have the keyword AFTER. To position our column in relation to the others, we will use the already existing columns. We will, for example, tell it to add the column after the x or y column. col_prec_name is the name of the column that will be used as a guide.

Take the example of the table dev_gbook. We will recreate the column gbook_ip in the same place it occupied before it is deleted. Tat is to say, after the column gbook_id and before the column gbook_msg.

We must, therefore, use the AFTER keyword, and the column gbook_id will be the reference since it is after this column that we want to place the new one.

The type of the new column will be INT (10). And zoup, mini-TP, it's up to you to create this request.

With a SHOW COLUMNS FROM dev_gbook, you will be able to check if the column has been created and if it is in the right place.

Now that our column is no longer in UNSIGNED, everything is fine. But bad luck, I'm really clumsy, and I totally forgot to tell MySQL that the column can not contain NULL.

Chapter Seven

PHP And Errors

Mistakes are many things that can spoil our lives. However, these errors are not unnecessary, and ensuring that they are properly managed is crucial throughout the life of an application. This will be the subject of the chapter.

Errors

Quite often, we have encountered charming messages from PHP. Here are some examples:

Code: Console

```
Warning: Division by zero in C: \ wamp \ www \
TutoOO \ index.php on line 3 Notice: Undefined
variable: s in C: \ wamp \ www \ TutoOO \ index.php
on line 4
Warning: fopen (lala) [function.fopen]: failed to
open stream: No such file or direct Fatal error:
Call to undefined function f () in C: \ wamp \ www \
TutoOO \ index.php on line Parse error: parse error,
expecting "("in C: \ wamp \ www \ TutoOO \ index.php
on line 3
```

You should not perceive these errors as boredom, embarrassment, or otherwise, but as a tool. Errors allow you to detect problems in your application, so they are very useful for improving your codes and making them more robust. Let's take a very simple example: we create a function to divide two numbers:

```php
Code: PHP
<? Php
divided function ($ a, $ b)
{
return $ a / $ b;
}
```

If a clever little has fun giving the value 0 as a second parameter, this function will return false, because a division by 0 is not possible. If the rest of the script is based on this result, big bugs can pile up, and even make your application unusable.

Likewise, if you try to use a function that does not exist, what consequences will this have on your application? What will PHP do if your script is syntactically incorrect?

It is, therefore, vital to have a mechanism that will warn us when these problems arise: errors. In PHP, there are two phases when executing a script, if I can say: analyzing and translating your code, running your code.

The most common errors in the first phase are usually due to a syntax error.

The syntax of PHP is clearly defined: we know for example that after a $ sign, we can find this: a series of alphanumeric characters which can contain underscores;

a variable, in the case of hideous variable variables.

In the previous code, we find a $ sign, but a semicolon follows it. This syntax is not valid; PHP signals it to us by emitting an error of type E_PARSE, E_PARSE being one of the constants which indicate a category of error. E_PARSE errors also terminate the script.

In most cases, error messages of this type indicate what PHP expected or did not expect as syntax. In the example, the error tells us that PHP was expecting a "T_VARIABLE" or a "$." But what is T_VARIABLE?

When PHP analyzes your script, it will start by cutting it into a token. Thus, the operator && is, for example, represented by the token T_BOOLEAN_AND. So, if we have this script:

```php
Code: PHP
<? Php
var_dump (token_get_all ('<? php $ a && $ b;'));
echo token_name (308) . '' token_name (278);
```

The token_get_all () function gives us the token representation of the string given to it, and the token_name () function allows us to translate the code of the token into a slightly more meaningful name. Certain symbols, the semicolon, and the assignment operator, for example, do not have a token, they are as they are. The list of all the tokens used is in the documentation. By cutting your script like this, PHP can easily check the syntax and warn you if it finds a syntax error, so you can fix it.

During the execution phase, errors can also be generated: these are so-called runtime errors. For example, using an undeclared variable or function will cause this kind of error.

Here are the error levels that you will often encounter:

Error type Meaning

E_ERROR alias Fatal error Runtime error which will cause the script to stop: calling a function that does not exist, for example

E_WARNING alias Warning Runtime error which does not stop the script, for example, a division by zero

E_NOTICE alias Notice Runtime error which does not cause the script to stop, the use of a variable which is not declared for example

E_PARSE alias Parse error Parsing error that causes the script to stop.

The difference between types E_NOTICE and E_WARNING is pretty "ridiculous" to me. According to the documentation of PHP, a type E_NOTICE indicates something which can be an error but which can also be normal. Seriously, how can we consider that using an undeclared variable is a normal event in the life of a script?

There are others, the complete list is in the documentation, but these are the most common. The types of E_USER_ERROR, E_USER_WARNING, and E_USER_NOTICE are practically equivalent to E_ERROR, E_WARNING, and E_NOTICE, the only difference being that the E_USER_ * errors are generated by yourself via a function provided for this purpose: trigger_error ().

From now on, the first thing to do when you encounter an error is to read it. When someone comes to ask on a forum why their script crashes and what this error means, it quickly becomes tiresome to repeat the same thing a thousand times.

After reading the error, it should, therefore, be understood. First, you determine the type of error, and then you see exactly what she wants from you. If everyone could read an error, almost no subject would ask what one or the other means.

Handling Errors

When an error is issued, it is caught by an error handler. Natively, this error handler does little except displaying the errors it catches, as we have seen so often.

The first thing, which is extremely important to note, is that it is not because the error handler does not display an error that it was not issued. The reason is simple: this error handler is configurable. For example, you can decide what types of errors this handler should catch, or whether it should display them or not. To define the types of errors that the handler should catch, we will use a function that you have already seen several times throughout part I: error_reporting (). This function takes one parameter: a combination of constants. Remember, when we saw the different bases and the bitwise operators, we talked about flags, that is, the combination of several numbers with the bitwise operators. error_reporting () uses this flag method. Thus, if we want the errors of type E_WARNING and E_NOTICE to be caught, we will use the combination E_WARNING | E_NOTICE. The error handler will ignore all other types of errors; however, this does not prevent the script from terminating if the error issued causes the script to terminate. Let's test:

Code: PHP

```
<? Php

error_reporting (0); // does not catch any 1/0 error; // E_WARNING, not intercepted, nothing is displayed error_reporting (E_NOTICE); // intercepts E_NOTICE 1/0; // E_WARNING, not intercepted, nothing is displayed

error_reporting (E_WARNING | E_NOTICE); // intercepts E_NOTICE and E_WARNING
```

1/0; // E_WARNING, intercepted if you want to catch absolutely all the errors, the combination to use is E_ALL | E_STRICT. I highly recommend that you intercept absolutely all errors.

To define if the trapped errors should be displayed or not, we will use the ini_set () function. This allows you to define the configuration of PHP without modifying the configuration file, which is useful if your host does not allow you not to modify it. The PHP configuration file, php.ini, is a fairly simple file that associates keys with values, just like an array. The ini_set () function will, therefore, take two arguments: the key to modify and the value to inject. The key that defines whether trapped errors should be displayed is display_errors. The three possible values are these:

On to display errors;

Off to not display errors;

stderr to send the errors on a specific flow dedicated to errors.

We will only use the On and Off values:

```php
Code: PHP
<? Php
error_reporting (E_ALL | E_STRICT);
ini_set ('display_errors', 'Off'); 1/0; // do not
display anything ini_set ('display_errors', 'On');
1/0; // display the error
```

To check if ini_set () was able to change the value of the configuration, check if it does not return false with the strict comparison operator.

Throughout the life of a project, it can be in two states:

in development, or in production.

During development, only developers and testers will be required to visit the site to test it, spot bugs, and the like. Obviously, therefore, all errors must be reported and displayed so that bug reports and corrections can be made quickly.

In production, everyone can access the site. It is obvious that visitors have no use for errors, so they should be hidden from them. In addition, certain errors can give information on your site, passwords, for example, which can lead to serious security problems. It is, therefore, more than necessary to hide all this from everyone's eyes.

However, while in production, your application may generate errors for one or the other reason. If visitors don't care about your mistakes, developers need them. You must, therefore, be able to save these errors somewhere in a file, for example, without making them visible to visitors. To do this, PHP offers two configuration options:

log_errors, which indicates whether yes (On) or not (Off) errors must be saved, logged in a file;

error_log, which indicates the path of the file in which the errors will be saved.

Let's test:

```php
Code: PHP
error_reporting (E_ALL | E_STRICT);
ini_set ('display_errors', 'Off'); // in production,
we do not display errors
ini_set ('error_log', 'test.log'); ini_set
('log_errors', 'Off'); var_dump ($ f); // E_NOTICE,
not logged ini_set ('log_errors', 'On');
1/0; // E_WARNING, logged
```

Go take a look in the folder where your script is, a test.log file should now be there and contain the error.If you generate an error with fopen () for example, PHP will include in the error an HTML link to the documentation page associated with fopen (). HTML in log files, it's useless and it makes reading

```php
Code: PHP
<? Php
error_reporting (E_ALL | E_STRICT); ini_set
('error_log', 'test.log');
ini_set ('log_errors', 'On'); ini_set
('display_errors', 'Off');
ini_set ('html_errors', 'On'); fopen ('lala', 'r');
// HTML code activated ini_set ('html_errors',
'Off'); fopen ('lala', 'r'); // HTML code disabled
```

It may happen that in a script, you need to know the last error issued. You can obtain information on this possible error thanks to the error_get_last () function, which returns an array containing the very precious information, or thanks to a somewhat special variable: $ php_errormsg. This variable will only be accessible where the error was issued if the corresponding configuration option, track_errors, is activated. Example:

```php
Code: PHP
<? Php
error_reporting (E_ALL | E_STRICT);
ini_set ('display_errors', 'Off');ini_set
('track_erros', 'On');
1/0;
echo $ php_errormsg;
```

In summary, the most important things to remember are:

you should always catch all types of errors; in development, you must display errors;

in production, you should never display the errors, but log them.

I have presented only the most interesting configuration options, in my opinion, but there are a few others, you will find them in the documentation.

Refine Management

The configuration options allow us to change the default behavior of PHP when an error is issued, but not everything is possible. We may want to handle errors so that the native PHP manager is not enough for us. Luckily, it is possible to remedy this by defining an error handler ourselves. The idea is as follows: between the errors and the interception by the native PHP manager, we are going to come and insert our error manager. So when an error is issued, either our error handler takes care of the error type and processes it, or it does not take care of it, and the native handler will take care of it.

A custom error handler is actually a function that we define as a custom error handler via the set_error_handler () function. This function takes two parameters:

the function that represents our error manager;

a combination of constants to define what types of error our manager will intercept.

The default value for this second parameter is E_ALL | E_STRICT. Therefore, by default, our manager will catch all errors. All of them? No. In fact, a custom error handler cannot catch the following types of error:

E_ERROR; E_PARSE; E_CORE_ERROR;

E_CORE_WARNING; E_COMPILE_ERROR; E_COMPILE_WARNING;

and most E_STRICT errors.

In practice, this is not really a problem, since these errors should either not occur in production, or require special treatment. It is, however, possible to call a custom function in the event of an E_ERROR type error, we will see that later.

This beautiful function will take four or five parameters:

the level of the error; the error message;

the file in which the error was issued; the line on which the error was issued;

a table showing all the variables accessible from the place where the error was issued.

```php
Code: PHP
<? Php
set_error_handler (function ($ type, $ msg, $ file,
$ line, $ context =
array ()) {
echo 'an error occurred: ('. $ type. ')'. $ msg.
"\not"
. 'in the file ' . $ file. ' at the line ' . $ line.
"\not"
. 'Background:'. print_r ($ context, true);
});
$ s = 'lala'; 1/0;
<? Php
set_error_handler (function ($ type, $ msg, $ file,
$ line, $ context =
array ()) {
echo 'an error occurred: ('. $ type. ')'. $ msg.
"\not"
. 'in the file ' . $ file. ' at the line ' . $ line.
"\not"
. 'Background:'. print_r ($ context, true);
});
$ s = 'lala'; 1/0;
```

If we change the error filter to catch only E_NOTICE errors, we will review the native error handler:

```php
Code: PHP
<? Php
set_error_handler (function ($ type, $ msg, $ file, $ line, $ context =
array ()) {
echo 'an error occurred: ('. $ type. ')'. $ msg. "\not"
. 'in the file ' . $ file. ' at the line ' . $ line. "\not"
. 'Background:'. print_r ($ context, true);
}, E_NOTICE);
$ s = 'lala'; 1/0;
```

TRIGGER_ERROR ()

The trigger_error () function allows as we said before, to issue an error ourselves. This function takes two parameters:

the error message, the type of error.

You can only issue errors of type E_USER_NOTICE, E_USER_WARNING, and E_USER_WARNING, and by default, it is an error of the type E_USER_NOTICE which is emitted. Example:

```php
Code: PHP
<? Php
trigger_error ('pouet', E_USER_WARNING);
debug_backtrace ()
```

When an error is issued, it may be useful for the developer to know the function call stack. The function call stack represents the nesting of the functions called. Example:

```php
Code: PHP
```

```php
<? Php
function a ()
{
b ();
}
function b ()
{
print_r (debug_backtrace ());
} at();
```

The stack makes it possible to precisely establish the path of the code traversed, which has led to the error. For each element in the stack, you have: the name of the file where the element was called; the line on which the element was called; the name of the function; if the element is a function, the arguments passed to the element.

Note that the include appears in the call stack. So we can now improve our error handler:

```php
Code: PHP
<? Php
set_error_handler (function ($ type, $ msg, $ file,
$ line, $ context =
array ()) {
echo 'an error occurred: ('. $ type. ')'. $ msg.
"\not"
. 'in the file ' . $ file. ' at the line ' . $ line.
"\not"
. 'Background:'. print_r ($ context, true);
debug_print_backtrace ();
});
function a ()
{
b (0);
}
function b ($ arg)
{
trigger_error ('lala', E_USER_NOTICE);
```

```
} at ();
Code: Console
an error has occurred: (1024) lala
in file C: \ wamp \ www \ TutoOO \ index.php at line
17 Context: Array
(
[arg] => 0
)
# 0 {closure} (1024, lala, C: \ wamp \ www \ TutoOO
\ index.php, 17, Array ([arg] => 0))
# 1 trigger_error (lala, 1024) called at [C: \ wamp
\ www \ TutoOO \ index.php: 17] # 2 b (0) called at
[C: \ wamp \ www \ TutoOO \ index.php: 12]
# 3 a () called at [C: \ wamp \ www \ TutoOO \
index.php: 20]
```

It's pretty, and to exterminate errors, it's very practical.

error_log ()

I told you that displaying errors in production is very bad. However, our error handler does exactly what not to do. To save your errors, you could use functions of your own with a large database or file backup. But if you want to save the errors in a file or send the errors by email, PHP offers a function: error_log (). In general, an administrator is happy when he is quickly warned of a serious error, so we will modify our configuration manager so that it saves the errors in a file unless it is an error of type E_USER_ERROR, in which case we will send an email. error_log () can take four parameters:

the error message;

how the error is saved, for example by email or in a file; the destination, be it a file or an email;

additional headers in the case of a backup by email. Example:

Code: PHP
```php
<? Php
error_log ('lala', 1, 'lala@lala.com'); // by email
error_log ('lili', 3, 'file.log'); // by file
```

To get the call stack as a string, use this:

Code: PHP
```php
<? Php
function debugBacktrace ()
{
ob_start (); debug_print_backtrace (); return
ob_get_clean ();
}
```
Code: PHP
```php
<? Php
function debugBacktrace ()
{
ob_start (); debug_print_backtrace (); return
ob_get_clean ();
}
set_error_handler (function ($ type, $ msg, $ file,
$ line, $ context =
array ()) {
$ s = 'an error has occurred: ('. $ type. ')'. $
msg.
"\not"
. 'in the file ' . $ file. ' at the line ' . $ line.
"\not"
. 'Background:'. print_r ($ context, true).
debugBacktrace ();
if ($ type == E_USER_ERROR)
{
$ method = 1;
$ dest = 'lala@lala.lala';
}
else
{
$ method = 3;
```

```php
$ dest = 'file.log';
}
error_log ($ s, $ method, $ dest);
});
```

Intercepting Fatal Errors

I promised you a trick to intercept fatal errors, thing promised, thing due. The idea is to use something inherent to fatal errors: they complete the script. The whole thing is to be able, when the script ends, to detect if it is because of an error. With the function register_shutdown_function (), we will be able to record a function that will be called when the script ends, regardless of the reason for the shutdown. The trick is to register a function that will check if there was a fatal error with error_get_last (), and act accordingly. Unfortunately, the functions relating to the call stack cannot be used on the functions registered as such, but it is always better than nothing.

```php
Code: PHP
<? phpregister_shutdown_function (function () {
$ error = error_get_last ();
if ($ error! == null)
{
echo 'fatal error?';
}
});
f ();
```

Now that you are experienced in error handling, if I see a single error on one of your sites, I will pull your ears.

This chapter is neither long nor complicated, but it is important, so be sure to master it.

Conclusion

In this book, PHP: An essential guide to learn the realms of PHP from A-Z. We introduced the most simple way to learn the realm of PHP. All the materials that we reviewed were carefully selected to inspire you to develop your acquired skills further.

This book should be considered as a starting point in your activity as a PHP developer. To develop your skills, you can use the resources we have provided in the reference section.

Reference

1. 2018. PHP is insecure by default Retrieved from https://learnwebtutorials.com/php-is-insecure-by-default

2. Connor, L. (2018). Introduction to PHP for web developers 2018. Retrieved from https://medium.com/employbl/a-developers-introduction-to-php-f8430572365c

3. Dann. (2019). The Future of PHP. Retrieved from https://medium.com/better-programming/does-php-have-a-future-6756f166ba8

4. Dipa, M. (2019). Starting With PHP - Installation, Syntax, Variables, Constants. Retrieved from https://www.c-sharpcorner.com/article/starts-with-php-installation-syntax-variables-constant/

5. Felipe, L. This is what modern PHP looks like. Retrieved from https://www.freecodecamp.org/news/this-is-what-modern-php-looks-like-769192a1320/

6. Full stack geek. (2019). 5 Articles, being a PHP developer, you should read. Retrieved from https://dev.to/full_stackgeek/5-articles-being-a-php-developer-you-should-read-21j9

7. IRYNE, S. (2018). Learn PHP with the Top 25 PHP Tutorials: Resources, Websites, Courses. Retrieved from https://stackify.com/learn-php-tutorials/

8. Jeffrey, W. (2008). Learn PHP From Scratch: A Training Regimen. Retrieved from https://code.tutsplus.com/tutorials/learn-php-from-scratch-a-training-regimen--net-60

9. Josh, L. (2019). PHP: The Right Way. Retrieved from https://phptherightway.com/

10. Krishnakumar, K. (2015). 10 Interesting Articles Every PHP Developer Should Read. Retrieved from https://codecondo.com/10-interesting-articles-every-php-developer-read/

11. Kristian, G. (2016). Step-by-Step PHP Tutorials for Beginners - Creating your PHP program FROM SCRATCH: Basic Authentication, Membership, and CRUD functionalities. Retrieved from https://www.codeproject.com/Articles/759094/Step-by-Step-PHP-Tutorials-for-Beginners-Creating

12. Matt, B. (2018). A Roadmap for PHP Learning. Retrieved from https://medium.com/@mattburgess/a-roadmap-for-php-learning-e7071b528424

13. Mayomi, A. (2017). Easy way to learn PHP: The beginning. Retrieved from https://medium.com/@mayomi1/easy-way-to-learn-php-the-beginning-5a60d600e3bd

14. Mike, S. (2011). Insert Statement With PHP Script. Retrieved from https://www.c-sharpcorner.com/UploadFile/c8aa13/insert-statement-with-php-script/

15. Mike, S. (2011). Working with PHP functions with XAMPP. Retrieved from https://www.c-sharpcorner.com/UploadFile/c8aa13/working-with-php-functions-with-xampp/

16. Tarun, A. (2019). Convert Array to String in PHP. Retrieved from https://www.c-sharpcorner.com/article/convert-php-array-to-string/

17. Vineet, K. (2012). Functions in PHP. Retrieved from https://www.c-sharpcorner.com/UploadFile/o51e29/functions-in-php/

18. Vineet, K. (2012). Insert Value FromCheckBox In Database (MySQL) In PHP. Retrieved from https://www.c-sharpcorner.com/UploadFile/o51e29/insert-value-from-checkbox-in-database-mysql-in-php/

19. Vineet, K. (2012). Mathematical Functions in PHP. Retrieved from https://www.c-sharpcorner.com/UploadFile/o51e29/mathematical-functions-in-php/

20. Vinnet, K. (2019). Dropdown List in PHP Retrieved from https://www.c-sharpcorner.com/UploadFile/o51e29/dropdown-list-in-php/

21. Vinod, K. (2013). MySQL Like Operator in PHP. Retrieved from https://www.c-sharpcorner.com/UploadFile/d9da8a/mysql-like-operator-in-php/